BOOK MAP TO AUTHENTIC POWER

The Seat of the Soul (1989)

The key book—about soul, evolution, and authentic power

**Thoughts from
The Seat of the Soul**:
Meditations for Souls
in Process (2001)
(with Linda Francis)

Soul Stories (2000)
Illustrates some ideas in
The Seat of the Soul,
and more, with stories

The Heart of the Soul:
Emotional Awareness (2001)
(with Linda Francis)
*In-depth explanation, experiential
learning, and practical applications*

The Mind of the Soul:
Responsible Choice (2003)
(with Linda Francis)
*In-depth explanation, experiential
learning, and practical applications*

**Thoughts from
The Heart of the Soul**:
Meditations for
Emotional Awareness

Self-Empowerment Journal:
Companion to
The Mind of the Soul

Each book is a stand-alone experience.
They are all perfect starting points, so use your intuition.

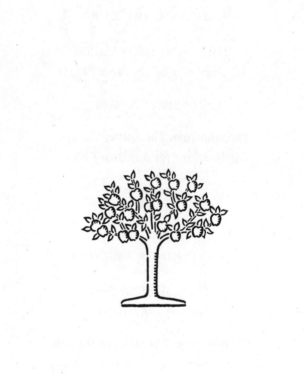

THE
MIND
OF THE
SOUL

Responsible Choice

GARY ZUKAV
and
LINDA FRANCIS

FREE PRESS

New York   London   Toronto   Sydney   Singapore

FREE PRESS
A Division of Simon & Schuster, Inc.
1230 Avenue of the Americas
New York, NY 10020

FREE PRESS and colophon are trademarks
of Simon & Schuster, Inc.

Illustrations by Melanie Parks

For information regarding special discounts for bulk purchases,
please contact Simon & Schuster Special Sales at 1-800-456-6798
or business@simonandschuster.com

Manufactured in the United States of America

1   3   5   7   9   10   8   6   4   2

Library of Congress Cataloging-in-Publication Data
Zukav, Gary.
The mind of the soul : responsible choice / Gary Zukav and Linda Francis.
p.   cm.
Includes index.
1. Choice (Psychology)—Miscellanea.   2. New Age movement.
I. Francis, Linda.   II. Title.

BF611.Z85 2003
153.8'3—dc22   2003055492

ISBN 0-7432-3698-X

This book is dedicated to my parents,
Teresa Compton and the late Hubert Compton,
with love and appreciation.

—Linda Francis

CONTENTS

ACKNOWLEDGMENTS

WE ARE GRATEFUL to Oprah Winfrey for her helpful insights and caring support, T. Byram Karasu for his kind advice, the Seat of the Soul Foundation for supporting us in our work, participants in the Creating Authentic Power Education program of the Seat of the Soul Foundation for their comments, Apryl Mohajer-Rahbari for her care, advice and support, Neale Donald Walsch for his title suggestion, Melanie Parks for her lovely illustrations, our editor, Frederic Hills, for his care and patience, and Carolyn Reidy, our publisher, for her vision and constant support.

WELCOME

THIS BOOK CAN dramatically change your life by showing you how to take responsibility for the choices you make and break free from the illusion that you are a victim of your circumstances.

Everyone knows that when you make a choice, that choice changes your experience. When you take a new job, move to a new city, or get married or divorced, your experience changes. That is obvious, but other choices that you hardly think about make differences in your life, too. For example, when you shout because you are angry, that is a choice, even if you do not think of it as such. Even if you assume that it is natural to shout when you are angry, that is still a choice. When you shout, you create particular consequences—people avoid you or start arguments with you. When you do not, even though you are angry, different things happen.

All of your choices create consequences, whether or not you think about your choice and even whether or not you are aware of making a choice. When you make a choice, you create consequences for yourself. That is why it is important to understand that you are always making choices, and to become aware of what you are choosing. If you do not make this effort, you will continue to encounter the consequences, and they may not be the ones you would want.

This book is about the power of choice and how to use it wisely. It gives you the tools you need to make responsible choices, and supports you experientially and in practical ways so that you can make responsible choices long after you have finished reading it. Our intention is to give you the most well-rounded, grounded, and practical introduction to responsible choice that we can.

This book is designed to be used, not merely read. The exercises, in particular, are important. Without them, you will still be able to understand the concepts, but they will not be nearly as useful. You will know more, but unless you actually choose responsibly, you will not change.

To assist in the process of meaningful change, we have also created a special *Self-Empowerment Journal* to accompany this book. It will help you focus your thoughts, emotions, and insights as you read and as you apply the exercises to your life. Of course, you can still benefit greatly from *The Mind of the Soul* without buying the companion *Journal*, but if you do not, we ask you to buy a notebook that you like to look at, hold, and write in, and record your discoveries after each exercise. Create your own exercises and write them, too—in whatever journal you choose. Most of all, experiment with what you learn and observe the results in your own life.

Last, we ask you not to accept anything in our book on faith, but to read it with an open mind and an open heart. If something we say strikes you as valuable, apply it to your life and see what happens. If you feel it does not apply to you, let it go.

Make your own choices.

Love,
Gary and Linda

PART I

Choice

1

THE POWER OF CHOICE

C HOICE EQUALS CREATION. **Each choice you make creates experiences for you and others.** Your experiences are dramatically and intimately connected to your choices. **In fact, the way you perceive yourself is a choice.**

HOW DO YOU PERCEIVE YOURSELF?

Do you consider yourself:

Beautiful	Ugly
Smart	Stupid
Handsome	Plain
Inferior	Superior
Competent	Incompetent
Outgoing	Introverted
Brave	Cowardly
Open	Closed
Emotional	Unfeeling

> Do you feel somewhere in between? Or do you feel one way sometimes and other times another way?
>
> Think about your characteristics. Write down the words that describe you. Take five or ten minutes to make this list.
>
> Now look at each word on your list and, after each word, say to yourself, "I perceive myself as _____ and this is a choice I have made."
>
> Keep this list.

When you choose to see yourself as incompetent, you create experiences of incompetence. When you do this consistently, these experiences seem normal to you, and you do not expect to have other experiences. This process is self-reinforcing because after a while, you become convinced you are incompetent, but that perception results from creating these experiences.

Choice = Creation

Your aptitudes and capabilities are unique. For example, you cannot will yourself to sing with perfect pitch, play professional tennis, or create a business if you were not born with appropriate interests and aptitudes, but thinking of yourself as incompetent because you do not have particular abilities and aptitudes ignores your strengths. You may be able to do other things well, such as sculpt, teach, create mathematics, or garden.

"Focusing on what you cannot do instead of what you can do creates a picture of yourself that is narrow and incomplete."

Focusing on what you cannot do instead of what you can do creates a picture of yourself that is narrow and incomplete. In that picture, you disregard your abilities, and you see yourself as incompetent because you choose to focus on some of your abilities—those you consider inadequate—instead of those that express your strengths.

When you focus on your strengths, you see yourself as a competent person because your desires and strengths are aligned. You are at ease. So if you try to develop a skill that you recognize is beyond your ability, such as perfect pitch, and do not succeed, you will not suddenly see yourself as an incompetent person. You will understand that the lack of a particular skill does not negate your many strengths. You will simply recognize your limitations and appreciate your strengths. That is why it is important to note the difference between recognizing your limitations and seeing yourself as essentially incompetent—and understand that this, too, is a choice.

A SECOND LOOK

Let's look at your list again. After each word, decide if you want to continue looking at yourself that way. If not, circle that word.

Speak each circled word out loud, one at a time, and as you do, say to yourself, "I can choose to continue seeing myself as ⎯⎯⎯⎯, or I can choose to focus on my natural aptitudes and abilities instead."

Most people think their experiences show them who they are, not what they have chosen. They do not know they have the ability to shape their experiences like a potter shapes clay. You are not the finished product of an unknown and unknowable artist. You are the artist and you are also the art that is being created. You choose the colors, where to add and remove clay, and you determine whether the art will be dark and depressing or light and joyful. There is no limit to your creative capacity.

When you identify with only a few colors and shapes, you arbitrarily limit your experiences, which is what you do when you make the same choices again and again. If you always shout when you are angry, or withdraw emotionally when you are frightened, you create the inevitable consequence—people push you away. They do not share their thoughts and feelings with you, and they cannot relax with you, nor you with them.

These are consequences of choosing to shout or withdraw emotionally when you are displeased, but they do not reflect who you are. Instead, they show you what you have chosen. You can choose not to withdraw emotionally when you are frightened, and not to shout, even while you are trembling with rage. Then you create different experiences. People appreciate you, and you inspire them. Individuals who are struggling with the same issues start to appear in your life and you support one another.

Shouting in anger,
suffering with jealousy,
and
withdrawing in fear
reflect
WHAT YOU HAVE CHOSEN
not
who you are.

Until you see that your experiences are consequences of your choices, you will think they are just or unjust, good or bad. You will experience yourself as a rudderless boat tossed helplessly by crashing waves. This is the experience of a victim. **When you**

"*You choose where to sail.*"

make the connection between your choices and your experiences, you do not have to create the same experiences again. You can create different experiences by choosing differently. Then your boat will have a rudder, your hand will be on the tiller, and you can navigate whatever waves come your way.

Each moment offers you an opportunity to choose anew. In other words, you no longer have to make the same choices you made in the past. **When you choose differently, you create differently.**

Your reactions to anger, jealousy, and fear are not the only reactions you are capable of. They are simply choices you have made so often that you cannot imagine choosing otherwise, but they are choices nonetheless. When you react angrily, you create the same experiences you created when you reacted angrily in the past, and when you react in fear, jealousy, or vengefulness, you do the same thing. You put yourself into a self-constructed prison where you will remain until you choose different responses. You are the prisoner and you are also the only one who can set you free. Which role do you choose?

SET YOURSELF FREE

The next time you feel an impulse to engage in a behavior you think you cannot change, imagine that you are about to put yourself in jail. If instead, you choose to think, speak, or act differently, imagine you are walking away from a jail.

Keep a log of when you put yourself in jail and when you set yourself free.

"... imagine you are walking away from a jail."

You may have been born angry but you do not need to die angry. Anger is a class in the Earth school from which you must graduate. Until you do, you will experience the destructive consequences of anger. How long you remain in this class is your choice. The need to please other people is also a class. There are many different classes. In fact, each of your emotions is one.

MY CLASSES

List the Earth school classes you are taking, such as anger, jealousy, gratitude, vengefulness, contentment, appreciation, or fear. Decide which classes you want to complete and which classes you love to attend. Put a check mark beside the classes you want to complete.

"the Earth school"

You continually make choices whether or not you think about them, and each choice creates experiences for you. Choices that appear significant create consequences for you, and so also do choices that appear trivial. You create consequences with your choices from your birth to your death.

Choosing is the act of creation. You may think you have no choice because, for example, your body does not look the way you would like it to look, or the person you want to be with does not share your affection, but nevertheless you must choose what you will say and do next.

Most people think carefully about moving, changing careers, and getting married. They research, analyze, feel, and use their intuition. They look at these choices as important because they know they are not everyday choices, yet other choices are even more important, and you make them each moment. **The most important choices you make are the choices about how you see yourself, the Universe, and your relationship to the Universe.**

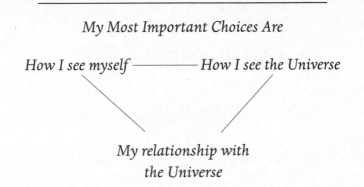

My Most Important Choices Are

How I see myself ——————— *How I see the Universe*

*My relationship with
the Universe*

When you see your life as meaningless, view yourself as insignificant and powerless, or look at the Universe as dead, merciless, or random, you create painful experiences. When you see your life as meaningful, view yourself as a loving, compassionate, powerful, and creative spirit, and look at the Universe as wise and compassionate, you create healthy and ecstatic experiences. No matter what you choose, you create experiences for yourself.

Your only choice is what experiences you will create.

2

CAUSE AND EFFECT

MOST PEOPLE THINK of cause and effect only in scientific terms. In fact, science *is* the exploration of causes and effects, but only physical causes and physical effects. No one could imagine all the possible physical effects of all physical causes, nor is it necessary, because scientists can use what Isaac Newton—one of the most famous founders of science—called the "laws of motion" to predict the physical effects of physical causes, and also produce physical effects by creating their causes. In other words, **a cause and its effect are not separate.**

What about phenomena that do not have physical causes or do not produce physical effects? They are excluded from science. For example, love, reverence, hate, jealousy, contentment, gratitude, and joy are excluded, as are your hunches, insights, the experience of meaning, and the content of your thoughts. Nonetheless, all of these have effects. Consider, for example, acts of kindness.

A WEEK OF KINDNESS

Go out of your way to be friendly and kind to people that you encounter during this week. Extend this kindness to people you talk to on the phone, email, or write. Then notice how you feel and what effects you observe in your life.

Science has contributed many grand and important things, from pharmaceuticals to space probes, but it is not designed to explore the things that are most valuable and worthy of your exploration. For example, no scientist can describe scientifically why he is excited about science.

Newton created the laws of motion about three hundred years ago, but science is a product of something much older—the exploration of the physical world with the five senses. Long before Newton discovered the laws of motion, early humans learned to use stones to pound, sticks to dig, and gourds to carry water, and with tools such as these they created shelter, clothing, agriculture, and, eventually, science.

Now the exploration of physical reality can no longer help us to evolve, or even to survive. Our experience is expanding beyond the limitations of the five senses, and we are becoming aware of nonphysical reality—intelligence, compassion, and wisdom that is real but not physical. We are also beginning to see the dynamics that underlie physical appearances, and as we do, we are becoming more interested in them than the appearances they produce.

"Our experience is expanding beyond the limitations of the five senses..."

In other words, the human species is becoming *multisensory*. The five senses are a single system whose object of detection is the physical world. The physical world is all that the five senses can detect, but multisensory humans can detect more. They have hunches and insights, and they see meaning in everyday circumstances, among other things. Within a few generations, all humans will be multisensory.

AM I MULTISENSORY?

Make a list of the ways you can identify that you are multisensory. For example:

- I sense what decision I need to make.
- I have hunches.
- I value my insights.
- I use my intuition.
- Sometimes I know more than I can see.

The goal of five-sensory humans is to survive, which they have done by developing the ability to manipulate and control external things. That is external power. Multisensory humans are not satisfied with controlling more or having more. Their goal is spiritual growth, and they understand power in a new way—the alignment of the personality with the soul. That is authentic power.

> ### TRY IT OUT
>
> Remind yourself that you are multisensory (you would not be reading this book if you were not). Say to yourself, "I will use my multisensory perceptions to see my challenges today as opportunities to grow spiritually." OR, ask yourself, "Using my multisensory perceptions, how would I use my life differently today?"

Multisensory humans evolve by creating authentic power. They know the Universe is not a dead or random arena in which Life happens accidentally, and they explore nonphysical causes and effects, in addition to physical ones. Millions of humans are now realizing that they are more than enzymes and molecules, and more than bodies and minds. They are becoming aware of themselves as souls, yet **the five senses cannot detect the soul.** In other words, humans no longer need to *believe* that they have souls because they are beginning to *experience* themselves as souls.

Multisensory perception is emerging in every culture and race and at every age level. It is a gift from the Universe that is appearing at the appropriate time, just as cognition—the ability to think and reason—was a gift that appeared in human experience at the appropriate time. Multisensory perception brings with it the new potential of an authentically empowered human species whose relationships and social structures are built on the values of the soul.

That potential is brought into being choice by choice.

3

THE SCIENCE OF THE SOUL

I T IS NOT POSSIBLE to understand responsible choice without understanding cause and effect, and science is the most complete study of causes and effects ever undertaken. Until now, however, science has concerned itself only with physical causes and physical effects. Multisensory humans are creating a new science—the science of the soul. **The science of the soul is not limited by the perceptions of the five senses.** It explores nonphysical causes and effects, physical causes and effects, and the nonphysical causes behind physical causes, which are intentions. It utilizes the dynamics that underlie physical appearances to create beneficial consequences and to avoid destructive consequences. Five-sensory endeavors cannot do that, because they can only manipulate and control.

For example, no war against war, campaign against hunger, or movement against exploitation has been totally successful because none has taken into account the nonphysical cause of war, hunger, and exploitation. The science of the soul deals directly with that cause, which is consciousness. The science of the soul investigates how to pull up the roots of war, hunger, exploitation, and all painful and destructive experiences permanently.

Five-sensory scientists think that physical reality shapes consciousness. **Scientists of the soul see that consciousness shapes physical reality.** The science of the five senses ends with understanding the relationships between physical causes and physical effects, while the science of the soul begins there and goes much deeper. It explores the larger arena of nonphysical reality.

"If a fool looks into a mirror," a saying goes, "a sage will not look out." In other words, a reflection will not change until what is reflected changes. Your experiences are a mirror, and your intentions are reflected back to you by them. The discord, competition, hoarding, and exploitation that surround you are reflections that will not disappear until you change, and you will not change until your consciousness changes.

A five-sensory scientist experiments in a laboratory by creat-

"What looks in... looks out."

ing physical causes and observing physical effects. Scientists of the soul use their lives as their laboratories. They prepare non-physical causes—choose their intentions—and observe the effects. You can become a scientist of the soul, also.

First, before you act or speak, become aware of your intentions. Second, consider the probable consequences of each of your intentions. Third, choose the intention that will create the consequence you desire. (That is a responsible choice.) Fourth, observe how your experiences change. If your experiences do not change, look for parts of your personality that hold different intentions, and change them when you find them. Then do the experiment again. That is the new scientific method.

BEGIN TO EXPERIMENT

Watch yourself carefully. Notice what you do and what you say, for example:

- Do you wake up grumpy or happy?

- Are you polite to some people and impatient with others?

- Are you doing what you love or what you would rather not do?

Begin to experiment with seeing each moment as an opportunity to choose the experience you want.

A war against a war is itself a war. War looks into the mirror and war looks out. The consciousness of war can create only war. Ending war in the human experience requires more than watching television and disapproving, or feeling shocked or hopeless, or political activism. It requires a change of consciousness. Until you change the consciousness of war in yourself—the consciousness of enemies, allies, villains, and righteousness—you will continue to create wars.

You will judge, criticize, blame, and attempt to change people. That is to say, you will create war in your consciousness. Human consciousness has created every war in human history—from the Peloponnesian Wars to the World Wars to the warfare that surrounds us today, including terrorism. Until you change the consciousness of war in you, you will live in a world at war. If you want the Earth to become a planet of peace, you must become a person of peace. That is how important the transformation of your consciousness is.

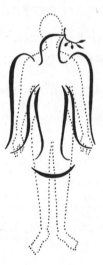

"If you want the Earth to become a planet of peace, you must become a person of peace."

Scientists of the soul change the reflection they see around them by changing what is reflected. **Changing the consciousness that creates poverty, hunger, and exploitation into the consciousness that cherishes Life solves those problems permanently.**

The science of the soul probes far below the surface of appearances and into the depths of intention. It utilizes the power of your creativity, applied with your awareness, and directed by your intentions. That is how scientists of the soul utilize the Universal law of cause and effect. When your consciousness is kind and loving, it creates experiences of kindness and love, and when it is violent, it creates violent experiences. When you care for others, others care for you, and when you manipulate with kindness, you will be manipulated, and so on.

LOOK IN THE MIRROR

Imagine that everything you see around you—the character of your friends, the experiences you encounter—is a mirror of your consciousness. Notice what you like and what you don't like. Do this until you feel you are getting to know your reflection.

Write in your journal what you intend to change and what you intend to continue.

When you participate in a cause, you will participate in its effect. The Universal law of cause and effect is called karma in the East and the Golden Rule in the West. Do to others what you want them to do to you, because they will. When you disdain others, they will disdain you. The more disdainful you become, the more disdain you will experience. When you love people, people will love you. It is that simple.

EXPLORING THE GOLDEN RULE

Remember a time when something happened to you that you were surprised and delighted about, for example, an unexpected gift or kindness.

Ask yourself, "Have I ever surprised and delighted others in a similar way?"

Remember when something happened and you were shocked and hurt, for example, when you were betrayed or someone raged at you.

Ask yourself, "Have I ever shocked and hurt others in a similar way?"

Note examples in your journal.

Scientists test their ideas by experimenting with them. Test the Universal law of cause and effect yourself, and see what anger creates in your life the next time you are angry, and what forgiveness, resentment, and patience create.

The New Scientific Method:

1. *Become aware of your intentions.*

2. *Consider what each of your intentions will create.*

3. *Choose the intention that will create the consequences you desire. (This is a responsible choice.)*

4. *Observe how your experiences change.*

5. *If your experiences do not change, find the parts of your personality that hold different intentions, and change them.*

6. *Do the experiment again.*

There is no limit to the number of ways you can experiment with the Universal law of cause and effect. Every moment brings you a new opportunity.

BECOME A SCIENTIST OF THE SOUL

The next time you are not sure what consequence your action will create . . .

1. Pause.

2. Ask yourself, "What is my intention for doing or saying this?"

3. Then ask yourself, "What will my intention create?"

4. If you do not like your answer, try another intention.

5. Choose the intention that creates the consequence you want.

6. Notice how your experiences change, or do not change.

You continually make choices, and you continually experience consequences of the choices you have made. This dynamic is already at work in your life. Now inject consciousness into this dynamic, and use it wisely.

That is the pursuit of authentic power.

4

ATTRACTION

I MAGINE THAT NEIGHBORS of every color are attending
a large block party and forming naturally into groups.
Which group would you join—the yellow, black, brown,
red, or white group? Most individuals feel more comfortable
with people like themselves, unless they are trying to disown
who they are. In that case, they are attracted to people who are
the opposite of themselves, or at least different. In general,
though, people identify more easily with those who dress, speak,
and act the way they do because there is a greater feeling of
safety in familiar surroundings.

In other words, individuals who share similar experiences
form collectives, each of which is a refuge for those within it, such
as the island of white students in a cafeteria of black students, and
the island of black students in a cafeteria of white students. His-
panic gangs, black gangs, and white, all-male, no-Jews country

clubs are also examples. So are social clubs, professional clubs, cultures, religions, nation states, and every "us" and "them" division. Collectives pervade the human experience. Within each are more collectives, and within those are yet more.

FIND YOUR COLLECTIVES

Make a list of the collectives you belong to, for example:

Mother	White
Student	Divorced
Male	Buddhist
Female	Businessperson
Christian	Black
American	Father
Wife	Yellow
Son	European
Asian	Daughter
Grandparent	Human

Beside each collective put a number from 1 to 10. Ten indicates you identify very much with that collective. One indicates you seldom think of yourself in terms of that collective. Notice which collectives you identify with the most.

Collectives overlap. For example, the collective of Muslims contains collectives of Americans, Asians, and Africans, among others, and each of those contains collectives of mothers, businesspeople, students, soldiers, etc. Each life unfolds simultaneously in layers upon layers of collectives. For example, one individual is Catholic, American, a mother, and a teacher; another is Japanese, Buddhist, a farmer, and a son; yet another is Brazilian, a student, and a daughter. Each feels comfortable with those in his or her collective, and less comfortable—or separate—from those who are not.

Individuals define themselves by their collectives. A white, American, Christian, businessman, for example, sees himself in those terms. When the collectives that an individual uses to define himself are different from the collectives of another, a gap appears. That gap is fear. The white, American, Christian, businessman relates easily to white, American, Christian, military men, and also to white, German, Christian, businesswomen, because they participate in most of his collectives. He relates less easily with yellow, Chinese, Confucian, businesspeople, and even less easily with black, African, Muslim, bricklayers. The more differences there are between the collectives that define individuals, the more fear exists between those individuals.

In other words, the more differences there are between collectives, the more fear exists between them. **The glue that holds collectives together is not language, skin color, belief, or**

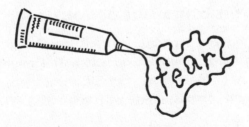

" The glue that holds collectives together... is fear."

common experience. It is fear. Within a collective is comfort and safety, while outside the collective is danger. Even violent collectives, such as gangs, alcoholic relationships, and abusive families, appear safer to individuals within them than unfamiliar collectives. Every nation, culture, race, and most religions, have a history of violence and exploitation, yet each appears safer to its participants than unfamiliar collectives.

The same fear that attracts similar individuals holds collectives together. If this were not so, cultures, races, and religions would have blended long ago, and individuals within them would relate soul to soul instead of black to yellow, white to brown, Jew to Buddhist, and Christian to Muslim.

That is why collectives cannot unify humanity, but can only divide it further. **The more frightened an individual is, the more he will identify with his collective, and the more violently he will defend it.** Nazis, the Ku Klux Klan, and fundamentalist movements, for example, are collectives of individuals who are so frightened they cannot tolerate even minor differences.

The attraction individuals feel to others like themselves is one side of a coin. The other side is the repulsion they feel for those who are different.

THE OTHER SIDE OF YOUR COIN

Whom do you separate yourself from? Take some time to think about this question. This might be a new way of looking at yourself and others, so be gentle and compassionate with yourself.

Write what you discover about yourself in your journal.

The appeal of safety in sameness is an intimate experience of the Universal law of attraction. The Universal law of attraction brings like energies together. It creates collectives of frightened individuals who reject the unfamiliar, but it also brings together individuals who are loving and open. The Universal law of attraction ensures that your values and perceptions, whatever they are, will be shared by those around you. It brings those with energy like yours into your life—frightened or loving—and keeps them there.

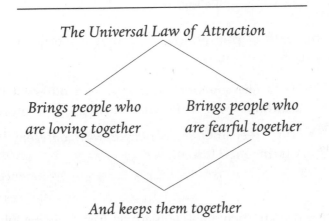

The Universal Law of Attraction

Brings people who are loving together

Brings people who are fearful together

And keeps them together

A culture is a treasure, but identifying with a culture is a prison. Your skin color is a blessing, but identifying with your skin color is a prison. When you assert the superiority of your way over others, that is fear, and when you value the ways of others as much as your own, that is love. When you love, collectives remain but the fortress mentality is not present, and **race, sex, and history become clothes you wear, not who you are.**

WHAT IS YOUR IDENTITY?

Are you attached to your:

> Nationality?
> Language?
> Race?
> Personal history?
> Clothes?
> Hair style?
> Habits?
> Religion?

Note each of your attachments in your journal. For each, ask yourself:

- "Do I feel superior to people with different attachments? If so, in what way?"

- "Do I feel inferior to people with different attachments? If so, how?"

When you are frightened, you attract frightened people and live with them in a world of fear. Not everyone lives in that world, but you do. In the same way, when you are loving, you draw to yourself loving people and live with them in a world of love. Not everyone lives in that world, either, but you do.

When you understand the Universal law of attraction, you can choose for yourself. In fact, you choose your world whether or not you understand the Universal law of attraction, and even if you do not know about it. If you are angry, you believe the world is angry and you are surrounded by angry people who validate your belief. If you are loving, you believe the world is loving and you are surrounded by loving people who validate your belief. Your experiences always validate your beliefs. Five-sensory humans say, "I will believe it when I see it." Multisensory humans know they will see it when they believe it.

CHOOSE YOUR WORLD

Choose the world you want to live in. Ask yourself questions like those below and consider them carefully, even if you think the answers are obvious.

Do you want to live in a world of love?
Do you want to live in a world of fear?
Do you want to live in a world of exploitation?
Do you want to live in a world of caring people?

Think of other worlds you want to live in. Write down each of your choices. Then ask yourself, "What can I do to make *me* the kind of person I want in my world?"

Write in your journal what you discover.

You can attract the type of people you want in your life by becoming that type of person. If you want loving people in your life, you must become loving, which means finding the parts of your personality that are not loving, and changing them. If you want to live in a world that is less violent, you must find the parts of your personality that are violent and change them. The process of change is not easy, but it is the heart of spiritual development.

"The process of change is not easy, but it is the heart of spiritual development."

When you identify with your collectives and fear people who do not belong, you attract people who identify with their collectives and fear people who do not belong. In other words, you isolate yourself in fear and attract others who are doing the same, and if you impose the values of your collective on others, you attract individuals who will do the same to you. This is the origin of war.

You cannot change your world by changing others, because **to change your collective, you must change yourself.** When you change yourself, you attract people with your new values and perceptions, while old friends and collectives fall away. For example, when you replace your anger with patience, you will no longer be attracted to your old friends who are angry, and they will no longer be attracted to you because you will have no further need of rage, but they will. When you replace your fear with compassion, compassionate people will become more interesting to you, and so on.

WHOM DO YOU WANT IN YOUR LIFE?

Pick three important characteristics you want the people you bring into your life to have. For example, "I like generous people; I admire people with courage; I want to be with people who have integrity." Make a list.

Think about each of the characteristics on your list, one at a time.

- How would someone with that characteristic behave? (What would that characteristic look like?)

- What would you feel around someone with that characteristic?

- What would having someone with that characteristic in your life mean to you?

Consider that to bring a person with this characteristic into your life, you will need to develop that characteristic yourself. For example, if you want generous people in your life, you will need to develop your own generosity. The same is true of kindness or courage or anything else.

Write in your journal the things you need to change or to develop in yourself to bring into your life people with the characteristics you want.

The Universal law of attraction shows you your beliefs, regardless of what you think you believe. Do you think you are generous? Notice whether the people around you are generous. If they are not, you are not as generous as you think. Do you believe you are caring? Notice whether the people around you care more for themselves or others. You need only see the people around you clearly in order to see what values and beliefs you hold.

You cannot change yourself by wishing, thinking, wanting, or desiring. You must change. When you do, you will cease to attract people who wish, think, want, and desire to change. You will step into a new domain of experience, and you will find new friends there.

5

IN-TENTION

INTENTION IS THE USE OF YOUR WILL. It is more than wishing about something, or wanting something, or even praying for something. It is determining to create it. An intention is a commitment to accomplishing an objective, to creating something that was not there, or to continue creating something that is.

Intention is the difference between having a vision and bringing it into the world. Inspiration is common, but inspired action is rare. The insight that illuminates a moment in the shower or occupies your thoughts while you daydream has no effect upon you or others, but using your idea or applying your insight does. The difference is intention.

Imagine a billiard ball moving across the smooth felt surface of a table. It continues in the same direction until it hits the side of the table or another ball. Until then, nothing affects its travel.

Your life is a trajectory through the Earth school that began when you were born and will end when you die. Like the billiard ball, it continues unchanged until it encounters a force.

The only force that can alter the trajectory of your life is your will to change it, but some individuals do not use that force. They remain angry, jealous, or vengeful throughout their lives, and they die with the same psychological and emotional characteristics they had as children. They react repeatedly in the same way and create the same consequences. Nothing fundamental changes between the time they are born and the time they die, no matter how much they might appear to have accomplished. They enter the Earth school frightened, and they leave it frightened.

Other people replace their anger with appreciation, or lighten up, or develop a sense of humor. Others learn to give, and still others learn to receive. These people leave the Earth school different than they entered it, because they are more patient, caring, appreciative, or insightful. Some change dramatically. For example, a young killer, sentenced to life without parole, becomes an elder to his prison community, teaching young inmates to appreciate the pain of others and respect the Earth. The model whose face is disfigured discovers appearance is not necessary to her fulfillment. The hoarding hermit learns to share.

Powerful lives like these surround you, but whether you see them depends on the choices you make. Choices that do not challenge your fears bring individuals into your life who do not challenge their fears. Choices that stretch you bring individuals who are stretching themselves into your life. **Choice is the power to make a difference in your life.** It is also the power to continue your life unchanged. It is the application of your will to your experience.

CHOICE
is
the application
of
YOUR WILL
to
YOUR EXPERIENCE.

You apply your will moment by moment. If you are not aware of this process, your experiences will not change, but once you become aware of it, you can change your experiences. **You create your experiences with your will, moment by moment, from your birth to your death.** When an infant who is in discomfort cries, it creates an experience with its will. It gets attention. Then it begins to experiment with its will. Sometimes it gets what it wants, and other times it does not. This process continues until death.

Each life on the Earth is an experience of the use of will, but in some cases, it is an experiment with the use of will. **The difference between an experience of your life and an experiment with your life is awareness of choice.** When consciousness is injected into the process of using your will, your *experiences* of life become your *experiments* with life.

Your life is no longer a passive experience—something that happens to you. Perceptions of good and bad luck disappear, and you think instead in terms of choices and consequences. **When you shift your orientation from a victim to a creator, your life ceases to frighten you and becomes interesting.**

VICTIM OR CREATOR?

List the aspects of your life that you are most aware of, for example, your . . .

- Job
- Partner
- House/Apartment
- Salary
- Status
- Race
- Cultural background

Ask yourself, one aspect at a time, which of the following statements feels more appropriate to you. Be truthful.

1. I wish this person or situation were not like this. (Victim)

2. I know this person or situation is perfect for me at this moment. (Creator)

Write a 1 or a 2 beside each aspect to remind you of your answer.

The first glimpse of yourself as a creator is a point of no return after which you may ignore what you have seen, or pretend you did not see it, but each of those choices also creates your experiences. **The spiritual path is not an escape from responsibility. It is a journey into the full depth and scope of your creative power, and your responsibility for it.**

The
SPIRITUAL PATH
is a
JOURNEY
into your
CREATIVE POWER
and
RESPONSIBILITY.

You may think about getting a new job, going to school, or writing a book, but until you decide to do it, nothing happens. You drift through thoughts of what could or should be, your job remains the same, you do not go to school, and your book remains unwritten. In other words, you have used your will to stay in the same job, not go to school, and leave your book unwritten because if you had decided to do them, they would be done. You decided not to do them, and so they did not get done.

Nothing is accomplished without intention—no yard gets mowed, car gets washed, or book gets read without a decision to do so. Behind every action is the intention of the actor. An intention is a quality of consciousness that accompanies an action. It is the motivation for the action. The action, such as seeking a new job, is visible and so is the effect of the action, such as finding the job. However, the intention behind the action cannot be detected by the five senses.

For example, some people change jobs to make more money, some to find more meaning, some to gain influence, and others to help people. Of those who seek money, some intend to send children to school and others intend to ski. **The action is not fundamental. The unseen reason behind the action is. That is the intention.**

Actions that appear the same can have different intentions. One individual may donate to a charity to obtain a tax deduction, while another may donate to help children. Their actions are the same, but their intentions are not. The first individual intends to benefit himself, and the second intends to benefit others.

You cannot see these intentions, yet the consequences they create are different because **consequences are determined by intentions, not actions.** The intention, not the action, is the cause. Every intention sets the Universal law of cause and effect into motion. Newton's laws of motion describe the relationship of physical causes to physical effects. The Universal law of cause and effect encompasses much more. It relates *nonphysical* causes— intentions—to effects. When you understand the Universal law of cause and effect, you will easily be able to see why the intention to reduce taxes creates one set of consequences, and the intention to help people creates another.

" The first glimpse of yourself as a
creator is a point of no return."

The Universal law of attraction brings like intentions—not like actions—together. When you intend to benefit yourself you will encounter others who intend to benefit themselves, even while appearing to be helpful, and when you intend to help people you will encounter people who intend to help you. Multisensory humans see not only the physical cause, but also the intention behind the physical cause, and the effect of the intention. They see the entire dynamic. This allows them to create the experiences they desire by choosing their intentions.

WHOM ARE YOU ATTRACTING?

Take a moment to think about the people in your life. In general, are they people who:

- Please others so they feel better themselves?

- Gossip?

- Love life?

- Trust the Universe?

- Don't understand why things happen to them?

- Want revenge?

- Are angry and shout?

- Are angry and don't shout?

- Give freely?

Create your own list so you can see whom you are attracting.

Write what you learn about yourself in your journal.

Your intentions determine your experiences, whether or not you are aware of your intentions. When you become aware of your intentions, you can change your experiences by changing your intentions. **The choice of intention is the fundamental choice.** You need only know your intention and the Universal law of cause and effect, and the Universal law of attraction will do the rest.

Most people think an intention is a goal. For example, an athlete intends to run her best race, a father intends to feed his family, no matter what, a sick person intends to become healthy, etc., but a goal is not an intention. It is an *out-tention*. An in-tention is different from an out-tention. **What most people call in-tentions are actually out-tentions. An out-tention is the application of your will to accomplish a physical goal. An in-tention is the quality of consciousness you bring to an action.** When you choose an out-tention, you choose a physical goal. When you choose an in-tention, you choose a consciousness.

An
IN-TENTION
is
the quality of
CONSCIOUSNESS
you bring to
an
ACTION.

An out-tention creates physical causes and physical effects. For example, graduating with honors, getting a promotion, and winning at tennis are out-tentions. The same out-tention can have different in-tentions. You can out-tend to keep someone off a boat because you know he cannot swim or because you want his place on the boat. In this case, the same out-tention will create different consequences because the in-tention is different. The first in-tention is to protect someone, and the second in-tention is to benefit yourself at the expense of another.

Sometimes when you think you in-tend one thing, you actually in-tend something else. You can discover if this is the case by becoming aware of your emotions. If you in-tended one thing and then are disappointed at the consequence, you had a hidden agenda you did not know about—an in-tention that was different from the in-tention you thought you held. For example, if you gave a friend a gift of love, and your friend did not accept it, would that disturb you? If so, your in-tention was to manipulate your friend. If that were not the case, you would not have been upset. You wanted more than to express your love. You wanted your friend to love you.

THE REAL THING

Remember a time when you in-tended something good for someone and the outcome was hurtful to you. For example, you gave a gift and your friend did not acknowledge your gift, or your friend ignored you.

Notice what you are feeling in your solar plexus, chest, and throat areas as you remember this experience.

Now ask yourself, "What was my real in-tention?"

Write what you discover in your journal.

When your in-tentions are the intentions of your soul, you attract others who hold the same in-tentions. Even if your out-tentions are different, you will be drawn to one another. A kind carpenter is attracted to kind teachers, kind students, and kind physicians, and a cruel carpenter is attracted to cruel teachers, cruel students, and cruel physicians. **Like in-tentions attract.**

MY OUT-TENTIONS AND IN-TENTIONS

Make a list of your top goals (out-tentions) for this year.

Beside each goal, write your in-tention. Take some time to feel what your real in-tention is. It might be different than you think at first. For example:

Out-tention	Possible In-tentions
Take a vacation	Rest yourself
	Impress your girlfriend
	Avoid a confrontation
Run a marathon	Improve your own time
	Impress others
	Avoid spending time with your partner
Get a new job	Be more creative
	Make more money
	Feel less stress
Plant a garden	Nurture yourself
	Save money
	Avoid your feelings

Write your discoveries in your journal.

Now that we are moving beyond the limitations of the five senses, the difference between in-tentions and out-tentions is becoming visible, and our evolution requires distinguishing between them because it requires aligning your personality with the intentions of your soul. **The intentions of your soul are harmony, cooperation, sharing, and reverence for Life.** In other words, our evolution now requires choosing *in-tentions* in addition to *out-tentions*. An out-tention will not create authentic power if the in-tention is not aligned with the intentions of your soul. The intentions of your soul will create authentic power regardless of the out-tention.

Five-sensory humans choose out-tentions and attempt to change their lives by changing circumstances. They are not aware of the Universal law of cause and effect or the Universal law of attraction, and so their circumstances change, but their lives do not. Multisensory humans use both laws. They choose out-tentions to create their circumstances, and they change their lives with their in-tentions.

PART 2

How to Choose

6

THE PERSONALITY

YOUR PERSONALITY IS a vehicle that your soul uses to experience the domain of the five senses. It is the part of you that was born at a certain time and will die at a certain time. It is also the part of you that becomes happy and sad, frightened and joyful, angry and caring. When you die, your personality will come to an end, but you will not come to an end. The part of you that existed before you were born will continue to exist. That part is your soul.

Your personality is your friend. As long as you are on the Earth, you will have a personality, because living on the Earth and having a personality are the same thing. You cannot discard, escape, or transcend your personality while you are on the Earth, but you can change it by learning from your experiences. If you do not learn from your experiences, your personality remains unchanged and your anger, resentment, fear, and jealousy continue to control you.

You experience the parts of your soul that your soul wants to heal through your personality. These are the parts of your personality that are angry, jealous, or resentful, feel superior or inferior, and so forth. Your soul does not experience the painful emotions that pervade your consciousness. It experiences a distance from Light, which your personality experiences as anger, jealousy, resentment, despair, vengefulness, inferiority, superiority, etc. All of these experiences are forms of fear, and they exist for you only while you are on the Earth—while you have a personality. They are the experiences you were born to encounter, and each provides you an opportunity to respond in constructive ways—to create authentic power. **Your personality is perfectly suited to the needs of your soul.**

Your challenges and joys, the decisions you make, and the consequences they create are all experiences of your personality. For example, you listen to music and read books with your personality. From your birth until your death your personality provides you experiences that are tailored for your spiritual growth, to assist you in healing the frightened parts of your personality and cultivating the parts that are healthy and wholesome. Your experiences show you these different parts.

THE PERFECT PERSONALITY

Quickly list some physical characteristics you were born with and you do not like, but that you are willing to see from a different perspective. For example:

- I hate my thin (thick/curly/straight) hair.
- I wish I weren't so short/tall.

- My poor vision keeps me from doing what I want.

- I wish my skin weren't white (black/yellow/brown).

- I don't like my brown (green/blue) eyes.

- I can't sing on key.

When you have completed your list, go back to each item and say to yourself, "What if this part of my personality were perfectly suited for my journey through the Earth school?"

Now open yourself to the possibility that this is exactly the way it is.

Your personality is a vessel designed for a single voyage. When the voyage is over, your soul discards it. All that is born, including your personality, dies. When you think that you and your personality are the same, you do not understand your beginning and you fear your end. Your personality is an exquisite, appropriate, complex, and temporary energy tool of your soul.

"Your personality is a vessel designed for a single voyage."

Your personality includes your body. It is male or female, delicate or large, brown or yellow, and it moves through childhood, youth, adulthood, and old age without respite. When you die, your body returns to ashes and dust, its destination. Everybody will reach it.

Your personality includes your intuitional structure. As you become multisensory, you become highly intuitive. Every individual experiences intuition in his or her own way. For example, some people hear sounds, music, or words, some feel sensations, some see colors, and yet others see things they did not notice before. There are many ways to experience intuition.

Your intuition helps you stay alive and safe. For example, it tells you to inspect your brakes in time to prevent an accident, or to stop at an intersection just before a truck runs through a stop sign. It assists your creativity—for example, it prompts you to miss a meeting so you can receive an important call. It also assists your spiritual growth. It is clarity when you are confused, and the unexpected answer to your question. All this information comes from the nonphysical world. In other words, intuition is the voice of the nonphysical world, and your intuitional structure is the way you experience intuition.

HOW DO YOU EXPERIENCE INTUITION?

Can you recall ways you have, or may have, experienced intuition—for example, knowing when something was going to happen before it happened, knowing what someone is feeling or thinking before they tell you, or seeing significant meaning in ordinary circumstances.

Open yourself to ways you may be experiencing
intuition that you haven't yet recognized.

Write what you find in your journal.

Your personality includes your intellect. The intellect and
the five senses are collaborators. The five senses gather data
and the intellect analyzes them. Intellect is the ability to think
and reason, which gave early humans the ability to recognize
that sharp rocks cut, sticks could be used as levers, and fire could
warm a shelter. In this way, it has discovered countless means to
manipulate and control external circumstances to enhance survival. That is its job.

Your personality includes your emotions. Emotions are
currents of energy that run through you, informing you when
you are learning wisdom through fear and doubt, and when
you are learning it through love and trust. When you learn
in fear and doubt, you become angry, jealous, resentful, vengeful, judgmental, critical, and in other ways attempt to control.
When you learn through love and trust, you are appreciative, content, engaged in the present moment, relaxed, and fulfilled.

Your personality includes your five senses. No personalities
perceive exactly the same. For example, some hear better, some
distinguish colors better, some have a keen sense of smell, others
are touch sensitive, etc.

All of these—your body, intuitional structure, intellect, emotions, five-sensory perceptions, and multisensory perceptions—
make up your personality.

You cannot give the gifts your soul wants to give while the

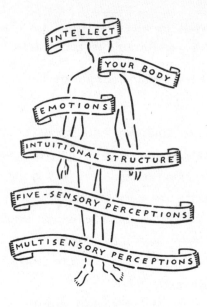

"*Your Personality*"

frightened parts of your personality are in control. For example, you cannot be angry and cooperate at the same time, resent and create harmony at the same time, or in-tend to win and to share at the same time. **As you heal the frightened aspects of your personality—the parts that compete, hoard, create discord, and exploit—you become more energetic and creative.** Appreciation replaces judgment, you become less rigid, and people become interesting to you because of who they are instead of what they can do for you.

Imagine your personality as a mansion with a different individual living in each room. Each has unique perceptions, values, and behaviors, and if you are not aware of the individuals, they do what they please. You may not even suspect that some of them are living in your mansion until you suddenly become an-

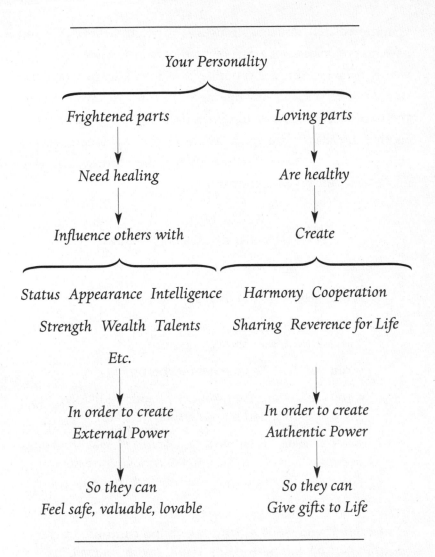

gry, jealous, resentful, or fume, withdraw emotionally, criticize, feel superior or inferior, or are compelled to agree or disagree, and a pleasant conversation abruptly becomes disturbing.

These are some of the ways you can encounter the individuals in your mansion. There are other ways, also, such as realizing you immediately dislike a stranger. You might believe that you have no prejudices, but a part of your personality does. Another way is realizing you are shouting at a friend again when you wanted to reconcile a disagreement. In this case, your agenda was to reestablish a friendship, but a part of your personality had another agenda. If you are unaware of the frightened parts of your personality, they will emerge when they choose, say what they please, and do what they want.

VISITING UNEXPLORED ROOMS

Remember a time when . . .

- You disliked someone instantly.
- You in-tended to say something tender but instead you said something hurtful.
- You ate to make yourself feel better.
- You felt close to someone and suddenly became offended by something he said.

Remember every detail you can. Think of that time as an experience of a frightened part of your personality that you did not know about, and that had an agenda of its own.

Decide if you want to continue being controlled by that part of your personality. If not, say to yourself, "I have encountered a part of my personality that is frightened and I have the ability to choose differently next time."

Write your experiences in your journal.

When you cannot stop shopping, eating, or drinking, or you cannot say no to sex, or you become angry when you want to be patient, you are under the control of a frightened part of your personality. **Your compulsive, obsessive, and addictive behaviors each show you frightened parts of your personality.** Your personality also has parts that are kind, patient, generous, loving, and trusting, that give, receive, and care about others. These are the parts that are aligned with the intentions of your soul.

Creating authentic power requires going through your mansion, room by room, and meeting each individual—those who hate and rage as well as those who love and comfort; those who are terrified and those who are fearless. Some of them you already know, others you have not met, and yet others you pretend are not there.

Each part, or aspect, of your personality brings with it conflicting goals, perceptions, and values. **Until you know all the parts of your personality, you will in-tend one thing and do something else.** You will see yourself one way and discover yourself acting another way. For example, you will be confused

"Illuminate the rooms of your mansion."

and feel guilty as one part of your personality after another comes forward, or you will strive to be compassionate but become offended instead. Whatever you choose, some aspect of your personality will disagree and you will find yourself angry, regretful, guilty, or resentful.

These are the experiences of a splintered personality.

7

UNCONSCIOUS CHOICE

WHEN SOMEONE "PUSHES YOUR BUTTON," a frightened part of your personality becomes active, and you do things you regret, such as damage an important relationship. You do not want to create damage, but a part of your personality that is angry, jealous, or resentful cares about putting someone in the wrong or getting what it wants, and you become righteous and rigid. You may want meaningful relationships, but while angry, jealous, or resentful parts of your personality are free to speak, you will not be able to create them.

PARTS
of your personality
that are
OUT OF CONTROL
=

BUTTONS
people can push.

Becoming aware of the different parts of your personality allows you to choose for yourself what you will do in each circumstance. Most people can make good choices when they are calm and grounded. Can you still make good choices when you are jealous, vengeful, angry, feeling inferior, or feeling superior?

NAME YOUR PARTS

Name the parts or aspects of your personality you know are out of control. Here's a clue—look for any automatic emotional reactions, obsessive thoughts, compulsive behaviors, or addictions.

Make a list in your journal. (You will use this list in the next exercise.)

You may know you are angry, jealous, or resentful, but not realize that you are also feeling other things. For example, when I joined the army I knew I was angry, and that I was frightened of parachuting and of dangerous missions, but what I did not know was how frightened I was of trying and failing, of being rejected, of not living up to my expectations and the expectations of others, and of being ridiculed. In fact, I was so frightened of these things I did everything I could to prove I was brave.

These frightened parts of my personality controlled my actions most of the time—they led me to enlist in the army, join the infantry, become a Green Beret, and volunteer for Vietnam. I would not make the same choices today, but I was not aware of them at the time. I thought *I* wanted to do those things. I did not discover how these parts of my personality were making choices for me until later, and then I began to make different choices. Until you have identified, acknowledged, and explored the different parts of your personality, they will make your decisions for you unopposed.

Here is another example: When Linda was young she also knew she was frightened, but she did not know that she was angry. Later in her life she began to experience how angry she was and how many things angered her. That was a surprise to her because, until then, she thought she wanted only to please people. Then she discovered that trying to please people was a cause of her anger! Now we both have more ability to choose our in-tentions and actions. For example, I still feel fear, but I usually decide not to speak or act in fear, and Linda still gets angry, but she usually decides not to speak or act angrily.

Your obsessions, compulsions, and addictions are also experiences of frightened parts of your personality you do not know about. Most people do not think of their personalities as having different parts, but until you come to terms with the different aspects of your personality, you will experience them through the consequences they create—which are always painful—such as damaging relationships and pushing people away.

Obsessions are magnetic attractions to particular people and things, for example, when you cannot get someone you dislike out of your mind. In this case, a part of your personality sees that person as the cause of its problems and will not let the thought go. When you cannot get someone you like out of your mind, that, also, is an obsession, because a part of your personality sees that person as the solution to its problems. This experience is very different from love. In fact, it prevents you from being able to love because you cannot see the person as she is.

When you cannot forgive a neighbor or forget an unfairness, you are experiencing an obsession.

An obsession can be shared, which happens when an individual adopts the fears of other frightened individuals and becomes very rigid about them. For example, he may need others to attend his church, read his scriptures, or salute his flag. His tolerance for difference is low or altogether absent. He feels superior because of education (or lack of education), skin color, or country. He is frightened of people who dress, talk, and believe differently. If you think of yourself as caring and, at the same time, you need others to be like you, you are experiencing a frightened part of your personality you do not know about. That part will not rest until its ideas, scriptures, beliefs, or flag are accepted by others.

GETTING TO KNOW ME

Refer to your list from the last exercise (Name Your Parts). Look at each part of your personality on your list. Give yourself whatever time you need with each one so you can see it clearly. As you consider each, say to yourself, "I am aware of you now, and I in-tend to remain aware of you while I make my choices."

Write what you discover in your journal.

A compulsion is the need to do something whether or not it is appropriate. For example, some people dress up when they leave home, even if they are going to the grocery store, while others eat their meals one kind of food at a time, because they become extremely uncomfortable if they do not. You may be late for an appointment, but even so you rearrange the papers on your desk, fold the laundry, and listen to your answering machine before you leave the house. You know you will be late, but you do these things anyway because otherwise you feel uncomfortable. The discomfort you feel as a result is the compulsion. Any activity can be compulsive, such as the need to buy more tools, clothes, or shoes than you need, or to own the latest technology or wear the latest style. **As long as you feel compelled to do something, you still have a part of your personality to get to know.**

Your addictions are the parts of your personality that are entirely controlled by external circumstances. They are your greatest inadequacies. For example, when an alcoholic sees alcohol, she drinks; when a sexual addict meets a willing partner, he has sex; and when a food addict finds food, he eats. An addict is a robot that has no freedom. A stimulus appears and the rest is automatic. Her life is an uncontrollable repetition of shopping, drinking, sex, eating, gambling, or whatever the frightened parts of her personality she does not know about demand. When you are under the control of an addiction, you will rationalize what you do. If you cannot refuse alcohol, for example, you will tell

"more than you need"

yourself that a drink helps you relax, or if you cannot refuse sex, you will tell yourself that you are a loving person.

Most people go from the consequence of one unconscious choice to another throughout their lives. They do not understand why they cannot keep friends, why they become ill, why they cannot finish projects, or why others do not respond as they desire.

Each painful emotion and uncontrollable reaction is a reminder to look inside yourself, not outside yourself. There is no other way to meet the unconscious parts of your personality. If a friend tries to point them out, you will become irritable, angry, withdrawn, defensive, bored, or feel misunderstood. If your friend persists, you will end your friendship or manipulate him or her into silence.

SEARCHING FOR UNCONSCIOUS PARTS

For the next forty-eight hours try this experiment: Whenever you react to anything, say to yourself, "I have encountered a frightened part of my personality."

Make a note of what you reacted to and how you reacted.

Describe what your experiment revealed to you in your journal.

These are experiences of unconscious choices. There is no joy in them, and there is always pain. **You will make unconscious choices until you bring the parts of your personality you do not know about into your awareness, examine them, and change them.**

8

CONSCIOUS CHOICE

ONSCIOUS CHOICES REQUIRE AWARENESS OF
IN-TENTIONS. While there are parts of your personality you do not know about, you remain unaware of
their in-tentions. When you become familiar with all the parts of
your personality, your knowledge of their in-tentions puts their
conflicts into the arena of your awareness.

For example, shopping during the lunch break appears to be a
conscious choice. But is it? At the same time you are considering
what you will buy, other parts of your personality are considering different things. For instance, a part of your personality may
not like your job and would welcome being fired. That part
might see a late return from lunch and an already-strained relationship with your boss as a way to get what it wants.

You are not thinking about getting fired, but that part of your
personality thinks otherwise, and it will make shopping seem attractive, remind you of what is on sale, and assure you the boss

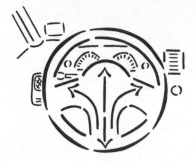

" You choose where you will drive."

will understand. If you were aware that a part of your personality would use shopping at lunch as an opportunity to get fired, would you still go? If you would not consciously make a decision to risk your job, yet you risk it anyway, was your decision conscious?

Knowing the in-tentions of the different parts of your personality allows you to choose among them, which puts you at the steering wheel. You can take control of your decisions, just as a driver takes control of her car. You are no longer a passenger who is driven first by one driver and then by another. Instead, you know where each of your passengers wants to go, but you choose where to drive.

DRIVER OR PASSENGER?

Remember an occasion when you were doing one thing while, at the same time, a part of your personality wanted to do something else. For example:

- You are at work and all you can think of is going on vacation.

- You want to be loving to your spouse but you are angry about what she said before breakfast.

- You love your sister but you feel jealous, remembering how she used to get all your parents' attention.

- You start a program you know will help you but you keep thinking about what you would rather be doing.

With this experience clearly in mind, ask yourself:

- "Where do I really want to go?"

- "Where do the other parts of my personality want to go?"

Then make your choice.

When you are aware of the different parts of your personality, they will still want what they want and you will continue to feel their desires, but your awareness of them makes a big difference, because you can decide for yourself if you want what they want. **When you are aware of what a part of your personality wants and you choose otherwise instead, you make a conscious choice.** You also challenge that part of your personality, and that is how you change it.

Until a body in motion meets a force, its direction of travel remains unchanged. **Every frightened part of your personality is a moving object in the sense that it thinks, speaks, and acts in frightened ways until you challenge it.** Then its path changes. The first step is to become aware of it—to recognize the moving object—because only then can you affect it. Until then, it affects you.

Again, you become aware of a frightened part of your personality by feeling the uncomfortable physical sensations it produces in your body. If you become enraged and choose not to speak in anger even while you are trembling with rage, you challenge the angry part of your personality, which is different from suppressing, repressing, or denying your anger. Instead you feel it, and then you decide whether to act on it. When you choose not to act on your anger, you challenge it with the force of your will and you also avoid the difficult experiences that part of your personality would have created.

BECOME THE FORCE

The next time you find a frightened part of your personality (notice when you become angry, jealous, hold a grudge, etc.), follow these steps:

1. Stop.

2. Notice where you feel this frightened part of your personality in your body—where there are uncomfortable physical sensations, such as in your throat, chest, or solar plexus areas.

3. While you are feeling these uncomfortable sensations in your body, decide what you want to do.

Every time you use this practice, record what you experienced and what you decided in your journal.

Imagine that you are at a large house party. Some of the guests are kind, some are angry, some are patient, some are jealous, and some are gentle. Others are so rude you wonder how they got invited. You recognize some of the guests but not others.

The house represents your personality and the guests different parts of your personality. All have been invited by your soul. You stand at the door greeting them. If you are not aware that each has an invitation from your soul, you will welcome some, ignore others, and still others you will try to have thrown out. On the other hand, if you know how special the guests are, you will greet even the loud, angry, jealous, and frightened ones warmly and want to know them better.

You are always at this party. It began when you were born and it will end when you die. If you welcome only the generous, gentle, and caring guests, the angry, jealous, and frightened guests will nevertheless be at the party, and they will continue to quarrel with one another. You can try to ignore them, but their conflicts will remain. This is what happens when you see yourself only as generous and gentle, for example, but ignore parts of your personality that are angry, jealous, and vengeful.

YOUR GUEST LIST

Make a list of the aspects of your personality you welcome and those you do not. Take your time. Consider, for example, the following:

Welcome Parts	Unwelcome Parts
Loving	Sloppy
Generous	Secretive
Playful	Jealous
Patient	Vengeful

> Now, one by one, imagine welcoming them as
> though they were friends. Notice how you feel as
> you welcome each. Note especially the physical sen-
> sations in your solar plexus, chest, and throat areas.
>
> Continue this practice until you begin to see all the
> parts of your personality as honored guests.

In the same way, when you see yourself only as quiet, you do not meet the parts of your personality that are loud, but that does not prevent them from speaking loudly, and when you think of yourself only as a defender of Life, you will not meet the parts of your personality that disregard Life—but the guests you ignore do not ignore you. When your buttons get pushed, they become angry, resentful, jealous, or enraged, and they ma-nipulate, control, shout, argue, and weep. **When you challenge frightened parts of your personality, no matter how strong they are, they begin to lose their power over you.** When you ignore them, or indulge them, their power over you increases, and they speak obscenely, behave cruelly, insult friends, feel unworthy or superior, hold grudges, or shyly hide. In other words, they do and say things you regret, and they create unde-sirable consequences.

After you meet all the guests at your party, you will know their perceptions, emotions, and agendas, and you will also be able to decide for yourself whether their in-tentions are your in-tentions. **You place your will between their impulses and your actions,** and then you can choose to say what you want to say, do, and create, and not what they want to say, do, and create.

That is a conscious choice.

When you know

ALL THE PARTS

of your

personality,

you can place

your

WILL

between

THEIR IMPULSES

and

YOUR ACTIONS.

9

RESPONSIBLE CHOICE

ER FACE WAS drawn and hollow, and fatigue etched eyes that spoke of struggle and a miracle. As I rushed to help her with her pack, she leaned her ice ax against the wall. Linda was home at last. I expected her long ago, and the thoughts that magnified my worry into fear and my fear into terror disappeared. She was too tired to feel relieved, but my joy was unbounded. The pack, flashlight, food, and water I was preparing to take in search of her lay unused on the floor.

Resting on the couch, she shared her story with me. Near midnight, twenty hours earlier, her group climb had turned into a solo ascent when her friends left her in the parking lot to wait for her climbing partner, who arrived late, unprepared, and too frightened to climb. Up the dark trail Linda hiked alone by moonlight, knowing that her group was ahead of her, but not realizing she would be approaching the summit before speaking with them again.

This was Linda's first climb, and the mountain she chose was higher than fourteen thousand feet. She had trained hard, but no training could prepare her for the fatigue, darkness, and demanding climb that lay before her. Near the summit, one misstep could send her sliding down a thousand-foot ravine littered with boulders. The darkness began to fade and tiny figures—her former companions—became visible in the distance above her. At twelve thousand feet she met them on their way down, where they chatted, gave her directions, and left.

Linda finished her climb alone, celebrated her first ascent on a summit three miles above sea level, and started down. The snow softened as the day became warmer, and she sat down in the heavy wet snow, pointed her feet down the ravine, and laughing with joy began to slide, first slowing her descent with her ice ax, then lifting it again to gain speed. At last rocks appeared on the snow, and she began to walk again, but soon loose stones were sliding under her boots, challenging her balance and draining her strength. The hint of a trail appeared, part imagination and part Earth, gradually took shape, and flowed downward.

The sun was low, but she felt certain she could reach her car before dark—and she would have, but for a single choice. Struggling to control her heavy pack and wobbly legs, she suddenly came to a fork in the trail. The left branch led to a small meadow, and the right disappeared downward through the trees.

"Down is better," she thought. That was the choice. In the disappearing daylight she walked past a small sign, fading into darkness, "Parking Lot .5 Miles," with an arrow below it pointing left. Linda turned right and followed the trail that disappeared into the trees.

"Where did you see her last?" I asked a member of the returning group, when she phoned me.

"About twelve thousand feet," she answered. "We spoke briefly. I was on the way down and she was on the way up."

"Did you tell her about the fork in the trail?" I asked.

"No, everyone knows that fork."

"This was Linda's first climb."

The phone went silent. We both suspected what had happened—tired and in the dark, Linda had taken a trail to a campground far from her car. At least, we prayed that she had. I thanked her and hung up the phone.

The night had turned cold and the mountain dark. I reached for my pack, ready to begin the search, and opened the door. There was Linda standing before me.

"I walked and walked," she said as I helped her off with her pack. "I knew I was on the wrong trail—the fault was mine—but I didn't have the strength to go back. At last I found a couple who were camping. They drove me to my car."

It ended as simply as that. Nine climbers had died on the same mountain in the previous nine years, and I was thankful Linda was not the tenth. If she had taken the trail to the left, the trail through the meadow, she would have been home before dark, but she took the other trail and a different experience came into being for her, for me, and for her friends.

In the same way, every choice you make brings a different

experience into being, and you cannot stop choosing, and, therefore, creating. Like Linda, you must choose your trail, moment by moment. **From the perspective of your soul, the choices you make are one with who and what you are.**

People who do not understand the magnitude of their creative power, and who do not use it consciously, see themselves as victims. They pray for luck and blame others when it does not come, bargain with the Universe, and see others as the source of their pain and joy. Their attention is directed outward, finding faults, advantages, opportunities, failures, and successes. They are tossed by their experiences like a leaf on the wind, going wherever it takes them in relief, fear, repulsion, and attraction.

A creator experiments with his life. He is like a sailor on the open sea, using wind, current, and stars to guide him. The winds are his experiences, the currents are his emotions, and the stars are his in-tentions—the choices he makes. No wind can blow

"He is like a sailor on the open sea, using wind, current and stars to guide him."

that does not fill his sails because he sees meaning in his experiences and learns from them all.

He rides the currents of his emotions—he feels different sensations in his body when he is frightened, content, jealous, loving, or vengeful—and he knows where and when they appear. Through calm and storm, waves and swells, he charts his course and checks it against the polestar of his in-tention.

You are always at a branching of the trail. Will you go left, right, straight, or stop? Which trail will you choose? What will you create?

WHICH TRAIL WILL YOU CHOOSE?

List a few of your recent decisions. They can be decisions about what you chose to say to a friend when you were upset as well as decisions about activities. Consider each one of your decisions as a choice of a trail. Think about other choices you could have made. Imagine these as trails you could have taken.

In a larger sense, ask yourself if the trail you are on now is really the one you want to take.

Linda's partner arrived late, unprepared, and frightened; her friends left her in the parking lot; and the trail branched unexpectedly—none of which she could change. She could only choose her responses.

A victim would have blamed her partner, judged her friends, and pitied herself. Instead, Linda is grateful for the lessons she learned. With her partner refusing to climb, she realized she

"Which trail will you choose?"

must set out alone or give up the climb, and she saw at the same time that she alone was responsible for her choices.

I AM RESPONSIBLE FOR MY CHOICES

Say these words to yourself, "I am responsible for the choices I make and the consequences they create."

If you aren't ready to say these words with commitment, try an experiment. Say to yourself, "I am willing to look at the possibility that I am responsible for the choices I make and the consequences they create." Repeat this three times.

When you repeat these words, notice what physical sensations you feel in the areas of your throat, chest, and solar plexus.

Climbing through the frigid night, Linda realized she could not overtake her friends, and instead focused on her next step, and then her next, eventually climbing the mountain that way. There is no other way to climb a mountain except step by step, breathing deeply, and resting often. In this way, Linda ascended an enormous height a few inches at a time.

From that experience, Linda learned to focus her attention and use her will, and the power of her in-tention took her a mile and a half toward heaven despite fatigue, pain in her legs, and shortness of breath.

On a dark descending trail, with no strength to climb back, her choice was either trust or fear. She chose trust and learned that she can always find her way home, however challenging

" climbing a mountain
one step at a time "

the path, or close and dark the night. She learned while climbing the mountain and while descending it. What journey could be more holy?

––––––––––

An unconscious choice is a reaction. It is automatic anger, jealousy, vengefulness, or fear, in which a frightened part of your personality does what it is accustomed to doing. Your reactions appear natural, familiar, and justifiable to you, no matter how they appear to other people. They are also predictable. When you are used to reacting angrily, for example, each disappointment triggers more anger.

A conscious choice is a response. A response is different from a reaction because when you respond, you detach from your upset, and then choose what you will do. In other words, you feel a painful emotion and, at the same time, *choose* your action. When you use your will to choose a response, you make a conscious choice. **When you choose a response that will create consequences for which you are willing to assume responsibility, you make a responsible choice.**

You can visualize, meditate, and pray, but until you are willing to assume responsibility for what you create, you cannot grow spiritually because spirituality and responsibility are inseparable. **Spiritual growth requires understanding the extent to which you are responsible for what you create.**

YOU AND SPIRITUAL GROWTH

You can do this exercise alone or with a friend you trust.

Say out loud, "I alone am responsible for my own spiritual growth." Repeat this several times.

As you make conscious choices in your life, record in your journal any changes you notice in your experience.

Responsibility and meaning go hand in hand. Without one there is not the other. **When you assume responsibility for your experiences, your life becomes meaningful and you become capable of relationships of substance and depth.** Responsibility is not a burden you must carry, but a doorway to your freedom. Without it you remain confined to your fears—

"Responsibility and meaning go hand in hand."

which are that you are unworthy, that others will discover your unworthiness and leave, and that you cannot live without them.

When you assume

RESPONSIBILITY

for your experiences,

your life becomes

MEANINGFUL

and

you become capable of

RELATIONSHIPS

of substance and depth.

Responsible choice is the healing dynamic that removes the power of your fears from over you. It is the way to use your life as it was meant to be used—to align your personality with your soul.

10

PULLING IT TOGETHER

IMAGINE YOU ARE a contractor with different potential projects on your desk. For example, an office building might be more profitable, but you feel drawn to building houses. Which will you choose? Your staff analyzes the market, but it cannot address your feelings, because only you know them.

Your mind is analogous to your staff. It reviews options and calculates, but it cannot tell you how you feel. That information comes from your emotions.

Another source of information is your intuition, which provides assistance from nonphysical guides and Teachers, from other souls, and from your own soul. Emotions and intuition are both interior experiences. Your emotions show you different parts of your personality, and your intuition provides guidance.

Most people use the first source, intellect, when they make decisions, but as you become emotionally aware, you will also utilize the second source, emotions. When you use intuition, the third source, you also access the compassionate and wise perspectives of nonphysical guides and Teachers. Multisensory humans use all three sources—they put their intellect in the service of their intuition, and they consult their emotions.

INTUITION

Can you remember a time when you knew you were making the right choice and yet you were very frightened to do it? If so, let yourself relive this experience in your imagination. Notice what physical sensations you are having in your throat, chest, and solar plexus areas.

Now remember your inner sense of having made the right choice. Let yourself become familiar with your own way of experiencing intuition.

Each choice creates external consequences, such as a new job, becoming engaged, or moving to a new city, and internal consequences, such as feeling at ease or feeling worried. You must live with both. **Which is more important to you—getting what you think you want or feeling good inside?**

Here is an example. Linda and I were on a plane and looking forward to working on the event we were going to conduct the next day. I had the window seat and Linda had the aisle seat in the same row. Our plan was to enjoy the empty middle seat and plenty of privacy. We had just settled in when a disheveled older man claimed the middle seat. Rather than be separated from me, Linda begrudgingly moved to the middle seat and gave him her seat on the aisle.

Before take-off, the man ordered a bourbon. He was unshaven and looked as though he had been wearing the same clothes for days. An invisible wall went up around Linda, and she could feel her chest area contract in pain. I noticed that she sat as far away from him as possible. Linda judged the old man harshly for these things, and also for depriving us of our privacy, yet at the same time, she felt an impulse to talk with him! For most of our flight she ignored it and felt righteous and indignant, instead of acknowledging what she knew she needed to do—interact with him.

Finally, with much effort, she turned to the old man, smiled, and asked him about his travels. He immediately told her that he had just come from burying his daughter. Linda began to cry. Understanding flowed through her like a river suddenly undammed, and she saw in that moment, at least partially, that she and the old man were together for a purpose. He needed to talk about his grief and his daughter's life, and she needed to recognize the pain that a frightened part of her personality created when it judged him, and how, when she did what she knew she needed to do, she created an opportunity to heal herself and support her new friend.

Linda's intellect judged the old man as unkempt and alcoholic. Her emotions created painful sensations in her chest and a sore throat. Her intuition kept her moving in the direction of connecting with him.

DID IT ANYWAY

Can you remember a time when you didn't want to do something and you did it anyway because you knew it was the right thing to do?

What did your intellect tell you?
What feelings did you have?
What was your intuition guiding you to do?

Write about this in your journal.

Your intellect tells you what you need to know about the external landscape your choices will create. Your intuition and your emotions tell you about the internal landscape they will create. For example, you may take a job for more money, but feel disappointed because you like the people and environment a lower-paying job offers. You may marry and discover you do not feel good about your decision, or that you feel better than you thought you would. Moving to a new city may be frightening but satisfying because you know you are ready for a change. That knowledge is information that comes from your intuition. Anxiety—an emotion—tells you about a part of your personality that is frightened. How much it will cost to live in the new city is information from your intellect.

When the thought of getting what you want makes you feel bad, it may be a signal that you don't actually want it. For example, you may think you want more money, but if you really want to work with supportive people, you will not feel good about taking the higher paying job, even though you are excited about the extra income. You will feel uncomfortable when you think about it, and even while part of you approves of the greater influence and larger office that comes with the job, you will feel heavy and burdened.

You do not need to feel heavy and burdened. There is another way.

" You do not need to feel
heavy and burdened.
There is another way."

11

INTERNAL LANDSCAPE

W HEN I WAS ACCEPTED TO HARVARD, the housing office asked me what kind of roommates I wanted. I asked for roommates I thought my parents would like, but I did not consider what I would feel after spending a year with people who pleased my parents. I got what I asked for, and by mid-semester I was miserable.

That year was difficult, but I learned to pay attention to what I create. Now I consider my internal landscape as well as my external landscape. I also learned that my internal landscape is the more important. I experienced this lesson every day for a year. You have a lifetime to experience it. **If you feel uncomfortable when you consider a possible future, your discomfort will not disappear if you choose it.** For example, if you are uneasy at the thought of marrying, do not expect that feeling to disappear after the marriage. If the thought of moving to a new

" You travel simultaneously through two landscapes."

city makes you feel content, expect that feeling to continue, even though you may feel anxiety about leaving friends.

You travel simultaneously through two landscapes. Your external landscape is the one in which you live one place instead of another, work instead of go to school, dine out instead of eat at home. The second is your internal landscape. Your external landscape may be appealing, but if your internal landscape is not also appealing you will not be happy.

Some people find an external landscape so attractive they ignore their internal landscape. They are sure they will be happy after they have children, become famous, or make a lot of money, but they do not consider the experiences that come with children, fame, or wealth. Some people feel good when they think about raising children, and the idea excites them. In that case, their internal and external landscapes are both appealing. Yet others feel imprisoned when they imagine having children, even though the idea is appealing. Their internal and external landscapes are different.

Here is another example. During our first year together, Linda offered to create a five-day participant event for me to present the concept of authentic power to a large audience. She had no experience producing such events, but I agreed and we set a date. Two months passed and she had not started. Then another month passed, and I became frustrated and decided to withdraw from the nonevent, but I held off. Then a fourth month passed, and by then she had only two months to organize and promote the event. I was accustomed to promoters who schedule events a year in advance.

I found one reason after another to abandon the project: Linda was not organized, I did not want to be associated with an amateur production, Linda did not stay on schedule, Linda did not have a schedule. Yet at the same time, I knew that I should not withdraw.

In the meanwhile, Linda discovered fears of failing and feelings of inferiority and helplessness in herself, and she confronted them. Suddenly she immersed herself in the project—she became organized, created schedules, and invited participants. People from throughout the United States and four other countries came to our event, and it was a startling success. It was also the beginning of the work Linda and I do together, including this book.

I knew it was impossible to produce an event of this magnitude in two months. That information came from my intellect. I feared association with an unprofessional production, or one that was poorly attended. That worry came from frightened parts of my personality. Yet I also knew that I should remain in the project. That came from my intuition.

My external landscape and my internal landscape were different. My external landscape—my dislike of unorganized events—was unappealing, but my internal landscape—my feeling that I should remain with the project—was appealing. However, that is not always the case. For example, when Oprah Winfrey invited me to Chicago for an interview, the external landscape—the trip and the interview—were appealing.

This pleasantly surprised me because Linda and I did not watch television and I was not familiar with Oprah's show. I felt no fear. In fact, I knew that accepting the invitation was appropriate because I had an image of a surfer in perfect position. The wave had arrived, and he did not have to wait or paddle to catch it. All he had to do was stand and ride. That was how I felt.

My intellect informed me about the invitation. My emotions revealed no parts of my personality that were frightened. My intuition gave me the image of the surfer and the wave. All was smooth and fun. Linda and I flew to Chicago, Oprah and I spoke for a few hours, and I appeared on her show a few months later. In this case my external landscape and my internal landscape were the same—all were positive.

Sometimes the external landscape and your emotions are in agreement, but your intuition is not. For example, an idea may be attractive and you feel no fear, but your intuition does not agree. No matter how you rationalize the idea and the pleasant emotions that accompany it, you cannot feel right about it.

When you base your decisions on your external landscape and ignore your internal landscape, you will create painful experiences, yet it is not necessary to create those experiences or to be surprised by them because they are there for you to examine before you choose. When you discover pain in your internal landscape, you can avoid bringing it into your life by choosing something else, and when you discover a beautiful internal landscape, you can live in it if you choose. You do that by choosing the option that makes you feel best inside instead of

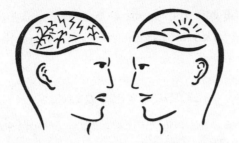

*"The internal landscape you traverse
is for you to choose."*

the consequences you think you want. You observe your emotions, listen to your intuition, and then make a choice.

Your parents or friends may or may not approve of your choice, but they do not live in your internal landscape. You do. They will never see your internal landscape, but you cannot step out of it. The internal landscape you traverse is for you to choose. If it has torrid days and freezing nights, *you* suffer—not others. If it has meadows, streams, and blue sky, *you* live in bliss—not others.

You can know in advance what internal landscape your choice will create if you take the time to look. You can explore the idea of marrying, for example. How does it make you feel—burdened and heavy or free and light? Take a test drive. Explore the internal landscape you encounter when you consider first one option, then another, and then yet another.

The thought of each option, such as moving, marrying, or changing jobs, creates experiences inside you. Just thinking about the possibility changes your internal landscape. That is how you can know in advance what internal landscape you will find after you make a choice—you can preview it before you choose. If you like the preview, you can make it your main attraction. If you do not like the preview, why go to the movie?

TAKE A TEST DRIVE

Test drive a possible future with your emotions and your intuition. See how you feel when you think about each of your possible futures, one at a time. For example:

- If you are ending a relationship you may feel pain in your chest and solar plexus areas (fearful emotions) and know that breaking up is the best choice for you (intuition).

- If you are thinking about changing jobs, you may feel open and relaxed in your chest, solar plexus, and throat areas (trusting emotions) and know the new job is the best choice for you (intuition).

- If you are thinking about getting married you may feel open and relaxed in your chest area (trusting emotion), but tightness in your solar plexus area (fearful emotion), and know that getting married is *not* the best choice for you.

Decide which possible future you will bring into your life. Write your experiences in your journal.

You do not have to dive into the water to see how it feels. You can put your toe in first by thinking about a possibility and, at the same time, paying attention to what you experience inside. Do that with each option you can imagine, and then make your choice. In other words, enter the reality you are considering, not with the energy of commitment, but to test the water. If you don't like what you find, you can remove your toe. If you like what you find, you can dive in. This way you won't plunge in and discover that, no matter how attractive the external landscape was, you do not like what you have created.

The process is always the same. When an option creates an internal landscape you want to keep, choose that option; when an option creates one you do not want to experience, choose another option. Choose other thoughts, other actions, other words. **Create the internal landscape that is the most nurturing, healing, creative, and joyful for you.**

PUT YOUR TOE IN FIRST

For the next few days try the following experiment:

Before you make a choice that stretches you (for example, not, "What flavor ice cream will I eat?" but, "Is eating this ice cream the healthiest choice for me?") consider each possible option you have. Do this without the energy of commitment. Just preview each option:

1. Think about it (intellect).
2. Feel the physical sensations in your solar plexus, chest, and throat areas (emotional awareness).
3. See how you feel inside about choosing the option (intuition).

Then choose.

Write your discoveries in your journal.

When you choose your internal landscape, you are not blinded by the attraction of a beautiful external landscape, nor are you blinded by the repulsion of an unattractive external landscape. Whether the external landscape is beautiful or bleak, you can experience for yourself the internal landscape you are considering before you choose. Then choose. That is a responsible choice.

You can respond to anything you encounter based on the internal landscape you want to create. When you choose responsibly, you become a gardener and your life becomes your garden. What you plant, you harvest. **Responsible choice is choosing the harvest before you plant the crop.**

"*Responsible choice is choosing the harvest before you plant the crop.*"

PART 3

Power

12

AUTHENTIC POWER

I N O R D E R T O understand authentic power, you must
understand that you have a soul. Your soul is immortal; its
home is nonphysical reality; it existed before you were born
and it will exist after you die. The part of you that was born and
will die is your personality. It is mortal; it will not live very long;
its home is the Earth, and when it dies, it returns to the Earth.

Your personality is a tool of your soul, but it is not separate.
It is a part of your soul that is on a mission to learn lessons and
give gifts in the domain of the five senses. When your soul discards this tool—when you die—your soul does not come to an
end, and neither does responsibility for what you have chosen.
The choices you make while you are on the Earth create consequences that, if they do not occur before you die, will occur
afterward.

Your personality is not the first that your soul has created, and
it probably will not be the last. **Your lifetime is one chapter in a**

"Your lifetime is one chapter in a book, and the book is your soul."

book, and the book is your soul. All of the experiences of all the personalities of your soul go into the book.

Many consequences that you create occur during your lifetime. In that case, a cause and its effect both happen between your birth and your death. Some of them occur after you die, and when this happens, they are experienced by another personality that your soul creates.

The lessons your soul wants to learn arrive in the form of your experiences. These are the consequences that you or another personality of your soul have created. Some were created before you were born, and some of them you created. Merely encountering a consequence does not mean that a lesson has been learned, but only that the Universal law of cause and effect has been satisfied.

For example, if you betray another, you will encounter the experience of betrayal. The person you betray, for instance, may be your sister, fiancée, or business partner. The circumstances in which the experience of betrayal returns may vary, but the experience will not. The anguish of the person you betrayed—her astonishment, disbelief, and heartache—will become as much a part of your experience as it was of hers. In other words, you encounter, in the intimacy of your own experience, each consequence you have created. How else could you learn so well that you change completely? **You learn from your painful experiences when you decide to change because you do not want to create them again.**

If you do not learn, you do not change. In this case, when you are betrayed you become offended and rage, shout, withdraw, or sue. You take the betrayal personally, wonder what you have done to deserve it, feel abused, and, in your pain, create yet more painful consequences. When they occur, you are presented again with an opportunity to learn. This continues until you make the connection between your choices and your experiences.

Your soul evolves as your personality learns. You are not a soul in a body, rather you are a body in a soul. Your personality is like a glass of water taken from a huge water tank, and your soul is the water tank. Your soul planned your incarnation. It decided you would be male or female; black, yellow, white, red, or brown; Japanese, Brazilian, or German; and all the other characteristics that define you and belong to your personality. But your soul is more than these characteristics.

When you align your personality with your soul, you bring meaning, purpose, joy, and fulfillment into your life. You forget to be frightened and you become fully engaged in the present moment, without expectation. You know you have a purpose, and all that you do serves it. People and the Earth become important to you, and your activities have value to you.

When you align your
PERSONALITY
with your
SOUL
you
create

Purpose   Meaning   Gratitude   Fulfillment
Connection to people   Connection to Life

Many people experience authentic power briefly—while cooking for a friend, sitting with a dying relative, or nursing a child, among many other things. Authentic power is the experience of having what you need and being content with what you have.

These temporary experiences of authentic power come by grace, and they allow you to see what your life would be if you were engaged in the activities that are most meaningful to you. You can also create this experience, but you must choose to create it. **Authentic power is your potential, but you must bring that potential into your life.** You do that by healing the frightened or painful parts of your personality and cultivating the joyful and grateful parts. In other words, the creation of authentic power is a process.

Every personality has frightened parts, including yours. **The frightened parts of your personality are not obstacles to your spiritual growth. On the contrary, they are your *avenues* to spiritual growth.** The consequences they create provide you with opportunities to learn lessons of wisdom, power, responsibility, or love.

---

*Your soul
wants to learn
a lesson
of
WISDOM
RESPONSIBILITY
POWER
or
LOVE.*

When you transform the frightened parts of your personality into parts that create with the intentions of the soul, you become a conduit through which the energy of your soul flows effortlessly into your life, and you become whole, healthy, and inwardly secure. You are grateful for your life, even when it is difficult, and you see compassion and wisdom in all your circumstances.

REALLY LEARNING

Remember an occasion when you were very upset, angry, shocked, or deeply felt a loss. Close your eyes if it helps. While you are reliving this experience, remember how you acted. Did you cry, rage, withdraw, feel confused, or become depressed? What physical sensations are you feeling in your throat, chest, and solar plexus areas? What actions did you take?

Now go back to the beginning of this experience in your imagination. This time, let yourself feel the physical sensations in your body before you took any action.

Say to yourself, "I in-tend to learn everything I can about myself from this experience." Give yourself some time. Then begin to pay attention to your life—to what people say to you, what you overhear, signs you see, and dreams you have.

Write in your journal what you discover.

Transforming the frightened parts of your personality requires your choice. They will not change merely because you want, desire, or wish them to change.

They will change only when you choose to change them.

13

CREATING AUTHENTIC POWER

Y OU CAN USE YOUR WILL TO MAKE CHOICES THAT
EMPOWER YOU RATHER THAN DISEMPOWER YOU.
For example, you do not have to act in anger because you
are angry, or withdraw emotionally because you are jealous. **You
can also make choices that create consequences for which
you are willing to assume responsibility, even while you are
feeling angry or jealous.** When you do that, you draw strength
from your choices instead of losing power because of them.

> ### MY WILL
>
> As before, remember a time when you had a painful
> emotional reaction, for example, you became very
> upset, withdrew and cried, raged at people, walked
> around confused for days, or became depressed.
> Really get back into that experience.

But this time you get to make a new choice. Go through the same experience in your imagination again and consciously choose one of the following:

- React the same way again.

- Feel the sensations in your body without acting.

- Feel the sensations in your body and act with one of the intentions of your soul—harmony, cooperation, sharing, or reverence for Life.

When you challenge a frightened part of your personality, it loses power over you and you gain power over it. Eventually, its power over you disintegrates, but that does not happen the first, second, or third time you challenge it. You must challenge it again and again.

CHANGE THAT PART

Pick a part of your personality you would like to change, for example, your . . .

- Anger

- Jealousy

- Resentment

- Judgment

- Anxiety

- Power struggles with your spouse, children, friend, etc.

Set your in-tention to heal this part of your personality. Watch when this part becomes active. When it does, challenge it by not doing what you usually do. While you are feeling painful sensations in your body, decide how you will act. If you choose words and actions that create consequences for which you are willing to assume responsibility, congratulate yourself.

When you challenge a frightened part of your personality, the Universe assists by providing more opportunities to challenge it. When you challenge your anger, for example, you will find that more and more things anger you. Friends will make irritating remarks, waiting in lines will annoy you, and your dreams will show you the archetypal roots of your anger, all because you have invoked healing and the Universe has responded.

If you become angry six times a day, challenge your anger six times a day. If you become angry twelve times a day, challenge it twelve times a day. You may not see progress immediately, but when you look back after a while, you will.

Eventually you will be grateful for your experiences of anger because you will realize, even while you are angry, that each provides you an opportunity to challenge an angry part of your personality. **Authentic power does not come to those who talk about it, read about it, meditate on it, or pray for it. It comes to those who earn it.**

When you have the courage to feel what you are feeling rather than act in fear, and then choose the intentions of your soul, you create authentic power. That pulls the causes of your painful experiences up by the root, and changes you permanently.

As the frightened aspects of your personality lose power over you, the healthy parts come to the foreground. You create authentic power by cultivating these parts as well as by challenging the frightened ones. **Responsible choice is the only way you can change a frightened part of your personality or cultivate a healthy part.** The frightened aspects of your personality are powerful and are accustomed to getting what they want. When you choose responsibly, you take command, and they can no longer take you in directions that you do not wish to go.

There is no accumulation of strength inside without making choices that stretch you. Perhaps you can easily say no to watching television, but can you as easily say no to sex, alcohol, shopping, gambling, eating, or drugs, or to your rage, jealousy, and fear? All your inadequacies come to greet you on the spiritual path so that you can identify them and change them. Each is a form of powerlessness.

Powerlessness is the fear of not being lovable, not being valuable, not being a part of Life, and not being able to contribute to Life. It is very painful. **Until you become aware of your experiences of powerlessness and heal them at the source, they will distort your perceptions, misshape your words, and determine your actions.**

Authentic power is using your will to transform your life.

FROM	TO
Experience ⟶	*Experiment*
Victim ⟶	*Creator*
Theory ⟶	*Meaning*

The creation of authentic power is self-transformation, through the use of your will, from a victim of your experiences to the creator of them.

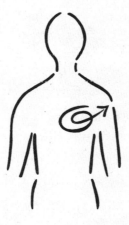

"Authentic power is using your will to transform your life."

14

ATTENTION

WHERE YOUR ATTENTION GOES, YOU GO.
When it is directed by an unconscious part of your
personality, you follow it. The frightened parts of
your personality look for what is not right, what you do not
have, and what frightens you most. They make comparisons and
find you lacking.

These perceptions served humanity while it evolved through
the exploration of the physical world because the goal of five-
sensory humanity was survival, and its means was external
power. The potential of five-sensory humanity was to create a
paradise on the Earth, in which every physical need is satisfied,
but five-sensory humanity did not reach that potential. The pursuit of external power has taken it as far as it can, and a multisensory humanity is now emerging.

Multisensory humans see themselves as souls, even while

they interact, work, and raise children. Their goal is authentic power, and their potential is a planet of individuals beyond nation, culture, religion, race, and sex. In other words, a planet of Universal Humans—citizens of the Universe whose allegiance is to Life.

The transformation of human consciousness from five-sensory to multisensory is happening from the inside out. Old challenges no longer appeal, and millions of individuals are finding new interests and new goals. This is happening in young people and old; in Americans, Nigerians, Koreans, and French; in businesspeople, housewives, pilots, and peasants. It is happening in crowded streets and in rice paddies. There is no place on the Earth it is not happening.

HOW ARE YOU BECOMING MULTISENSORY?

List the ways you have discovered that you are more than five-sensory. For example, I am . . .

- Reading this book.

- Interested in my in-tentions.

- Suspecting/sensing I am more than a mind and body.

- Becoming intuitive.

- Discovering meaning in ordinary experiences.

Multisensory perception is not new. In fact, most religions are named after multisensory humans, but never before has humanity as a whole experienced this transformation. Within a few generations, the entire human species will be multisensory. The rapidly changing experience of what it means to be a female is part of this transformation, as is the rapidly changing experience of what it means to be a male. Multisensory perception is expanding human consciousness whether or not we want it, and even whether or not we like it.

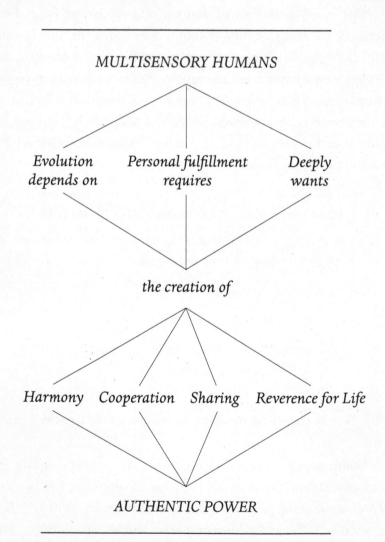

MULTISENSORY HUMANS

Evolution depends on   Personal fulfillment requires   Deeply wants

the creation of

Harmony   Cooperation   Sharing   Reverence for Life

AUTHENTIC POWER

A few generations is a short time compared to the history of the Earth. From that perspective, multisensory perception is exploding into the human experience, and with it the understanding of power as the alignment of the personality with the soul.

The conflict between the values of five-sensory humans in pursuit of external power and the values of emerging multisensory humans in pursuit of authentic power is occurring within all of us. In other words, **the frightened parts of your personality that focus on what is not right, what you do not have, and what you fear most are in conflict with the parts of your personality that focus on the intentions of the soul.**

When you focus your attention on what you lack, judge, or fear, you lose power. **When you focus on what nurtures, sustains, and feeds you, you gain power.**

TRACKING YOUR ATTENTION

For the next day or two, observe where your attention goes. Note whether it is focused on thoughts, words, and actions that come from fear and doubt, or love and trust. This will take some discipline. It will help to carry your *Self-Empowerment Journal* or a small notepad with you.

As much as possible, write very briefly each thought you notice, and beside it jot "love" or "fear." Keeping this log will give you a sample of where your attention is going.

When you find yourself judging others, you are choosing in fear and doubt. You feel superior, compelled, and you push people away who think and act differently. When you listen with patience and appreciation, even when you disagree, you are choosing in love and trust. You are flexible, you strive to understand, and you look for constructive, positive characteristics. When you choose in fear and doubt, you lose power, and when you choose in love and trust, you gain power.

In other words, **you challenge the frightened parts of your personality by choosing where you will put your attention.** For example, when you feel overwhelmed you can focus on what overwhelms you or what calms you. Similarly, you can tell yourself that your experiences are unfair or that they are opportunities to learn about yourself; and you can see yourself as a victim of your experiences or the creator of them.

If you cannot see how you created an experience, ask yourself, "How did I create this?" This question automatically requires that you consider the possibility that even your most painful experiences are gifts that you do not yet recognize, and when you ask it with an open heart and mind, you begin the

"... consider the possibility that even your most painful experiences are gifts you do not yet recognize ... "

process of creating authentic power. Pain is merely pain, but suffering is pain for a worthy cause. What is more worthy than your becoming the wise and compassionate, powerful and creative spirit that you are?

SOUL PERSPECTIVE

Remember a painful event that you still feel was unfair, but that you would now like to understand in a different way.

For this practice, assume the Universe is wise and compassionate.

Ask yourself, "Why would a compassionate and wise Universe help me create this experience?"

Then ask yourself, "What have I gained—what strengths have I developed, or could I develop—from this experience?"

Open yourself to answers, and remain open until they come. They may not come immediately, or in ways you expect.

Write your experiences in your journal.

When you ask, "Why me?" without self-pity, you open yourself to the perspective of your soul.

When you ask, "Why me?" with self-blame and judgment of others, you invoke the least powerful and most painful parts of your personality. You ask to experience their perceptions, thoughts, and emotions, and you nourish the parts of your personality that most need challenging.

WHERE YOUR ATTENTION GOES

Do this practice in real time. Notice the next time you encounter something that always makes you irritated, impatient, angry, judgmental, jealous, etc. For example:

- When I am in a long line at the bank I get angry.
- My spouse is never ready on time and I always get irritated and impatient.

Consider how you could respond differently.

Then choose how you will respond.

Consider this experiment each time the occasion arises.

Focus your attention where it will do the most good. In order to choose where you will focus your attention next, you must know where it is now. For example, if you are feeling overwhelmed, notice what physical sensations you are experiencing and what thoughts you are having, and as you do, choose where you want to focus your attention next. In other words, after you experience an emotion—and especially a painful emotion—you are free to either leave your attention on it or move it somewhere else.

EXPERIMENT WITH YOUR ATTENTION

Try this practice from time to time.

- Experience where you are now.
- Move your attention where you want it to go.
- Experience that new place.
- Decide how long you will stay there.

15

HOW TO CHALLENGE

NO ONE EXPECTED our granddaughter, four years old, to ride her bicycle on the first try. We cheered as she pedaled past us, shouting, "Look at me! Look at me!"

Her seven-year-old sister sat sadly on the lawn, staring at the grass and then at her hands, which moved nervously.

"What is the matter?" Linda asked gently.

"No one notices me," she finally said.

"That doesn't feel good, does it?"

She nodded her agreement.

"But you don't have to sit here alone if you don't want to," continued Linda. "Even though you are feeling sad, you can congratulate your sister and see what you feel when you do."

She thought a while, then ran over to her sister and said, "You really did a good job!" and they both laughed.

Later she exclaimed to Linda, "I don't feel sad anymore!"

At seven years, she learned a lesson about emotions and choice, and she was delighted. When she stopped thinking about her sadness and congratulated her sister, her jealousy disappeared.

This was her first experience challenging a part of her personality, in this case, a part that needed to be admired and was uncomfortable when it was not noticed. She did not consciously think about challenging a part of her personality, but she did that, anyway. You can do the same thing, and you do not need someone to remind you to shift your attention, change your in-tention, and try something else. You can remember that yourself when you feel a painful emotion.

SHIFT YOUR ATTENTION

Any time you feel emotions that are painful to you, such as anger, jealousy, sadness, fear, etc., remember to shift your attention, change your in-tention, and try something else.

Keep notes of your practice in your journal.

You challenge a frightened part of your personality by allowing yourself to feel it fully, and *while you are feeling it fully*, choose not to act in anger, jealousy, fear, etc. For example, you challenge your anger by allowing yourself to feel it fully, and *while you are feeling it fully*, choose not to act in anger. Similarly, you challenge your jealousy by allowing yourself to feel it fully, and *while you are feeling it fully*, choose not to act jealously. You can challenge any painful emotion this way: Allow yourself to experience it as fully as you can, and while you are experiencing it, choose not to speak or act on what you feel.

A challenge is an in-tention to change yourself for the better. You recognize an inadequacy in yourself and determine to correct it—to use your will to reshape your personality. When you do that, you reshape your experience.

When I was in the army, I was not permitted to express anger to a superior officer. I could become angry with someone of lower rank, but he was not permitted to express anger to me. Neither of us could express anger to a superior officer, but our anger remained. This is not challenging anger. It is an example of controlling yourself because of fear. When you do that, your anger continues and eventually, it explodes onto other people, just as mine exploded onto men with a lower rank.

Challenging your anger means not acting or speaking in anger because you are no longer willing to be dominated by your anger, not because you fear punishment. Containing your anger because you fear punishment is the pursuit of external power—you control your behavior to keep yourself safe. Not expressing anger because you no longer want the experience of anger in your life is the pursuit of authentic power—you use your will to change yourself, not someone else, by placing your attention on your internal experiences and not on what you think is causing them.

When you change your internal experiences, you do not have to change your external circumstances repeatedly. You need only change yourself once. **You challenge a part of your personality when you use your will to change yourself.** For example, you challenge a part of your personality that is angry when you decide not to speak in anger, even while you are trembling with rage, because you want to change yourself. You may think nothing in you changes because you are still angry, but everything changes. Before, you attracted people who act angrily when they are angry, and after, you attract individuals who are determined not to act in anger, even when they are angry. Which people do you want to attract?

When you challenge a part of your personality in order to change yourself, you create the freedom to choose the most constructive response instead of the most habitual reaction. Our granddaughter experimented, as Linda suggested, and was surprised. You can experiment, too, by shifting your attention and changing your in-tention when you feel a painful emotion. That emotion is calling your attention to a frightened part of your personality so that you can heal it.

CHALLENGE IT

Select an aspect of your personality that is frightened—in other words, a part that is angry, sad, disappointed, jealous, etc.—that you would like to change.

Each time this part of your personality returns, notice what physical sensations you feel in your throat, chest, and solar plexus areas.

Ask yourself, "What would be the most constructive response I could choose?"

Keep a log of your progress.

Credit your progress for even small steps. For example, when you notice you are angry and stop to feel the sensations in your body—even for a few seconds—before you create your usual reaction, celebrate your awareness and in-tention to change.

There is no other way to leave behind the tormenting experiences of the frightened parts of your personality—to remove the agony of your painful emotions. If you are angry or jealous now, what makes you think you will die less angry or jealous if you do not change yourself? Millions of individuals die angry, jealous, or vengeful. You cannot change yourself without challenging the parts of your personality that you want to change.

When those parts go unchallenged, they go unchanged.

16

AUTHENTIC NEEDS

Y OUR SENSE OF MEANING, like a compass needle, always points in the direction your soul wants to go. The more closely you follow it the more meaning you experience, and when you ignore it, meaning drains from your life.

Your internal compass can help you distinguish authentic needs from artificial needs. **Authentic needs are the needs of your soul,** such as using your creativity. When you give your most meaningful gifts, they will fulfill you, and when you do not, they will torment you because the love you give to others is the love they give to you. If you do not give love, you cannot receive love, and you will begin to wither.

GIVING AND RECEIVING LOVE

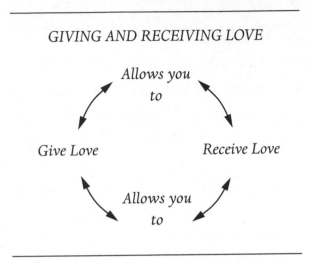

The need to communicate with your nonphysical Teachers is an authentic need because they offer you a perspective of compassion and wisdom that the five senses and your intellect cannot provide. Creating authentic power is also a need of your soul. In fact, it was the reason you were born. In other words, the more you use your creativity responsibly, love and receive love, and create with the intentions of your soul, the more you become a whole and healthy human.

Artificial needs come from the frightened parts of your personality. They are the needs you use to gain notice or prestige, or in other ways make yourself feel valuable and safe, and they become increasingly important to you when you feel powerless. For example, you may insist that a neighbor make less noise, a clerk be more polite, or a classmate be more respectful. You feel powerless, and instead of addressing the issue of your powerlessness directly, you create a need to address it for you. This is the pursuit of external power.

AUTHENTIC NEEDS	ARTIFICIAL NEEDS
Needs of the soul	Needs of the personality
Align personality and soul	Manipulate and control
Creativity serves the soul	Envy creativity of others
Love and be loved	Strive to be safe and valuable
Life fills with meaning	Life empties of meaning
Create healing, constructive consequences	Create painful, destructive consequences
Give gifts of the soul	Insist on being right
Fear disappears	Life filled with fear
Attract others who pursue authentic needs	Attract others who pursue artificial needs
Create authentic power	Create external power

When you can recognize the difference between your authentic needs and your artificial needs, you will develop a natural give and take and become more flexible.

AUTHENTIC NEED OR ARTIFICIAL NEED?

Remember the last few times you had a painful emotional reaction. It may have been a power struggle with your spouse or child or friend, anger at a slow driver, impatience with a long line at the grocery store, disapproval of some food you were served, etc.

Describe each circumstance briefly in your journal. Look closely at what you wanted or thought you needed in each situation. Now consider each item on your list and ask yourself if that need was an authentic need or an artificial need.

Write what you discover in your journal.

When you pursue authentic needs, your life becomes meaningful, but when you are satisfying artificial needs, your life becomes empty. That is how using your inner compass can help you distinguish between the two.

REASSESSMENT

Make a list of some things you would like, for example:

- A new car
- A meaningful job
- A thoughtful spouse
- A child

Review each, one at a time, and ask yourself, "Is this a need of my soul or a need of my personality?"

Now make a list of the things you have that are most important to you, such as:

- My values
- My children
- My wardrobe

Review each of these and ask yourself, "Is this a need of my soul or a need of my personality?"

Record your answers in your journal.

To create authentic power you must use your painful experiences as they were meant to be used—to discover what you need to heal in yourself. For example, if you become angry at someone, look in yourself instead of at the person who triggers your anger, and, if you look carefully enough, you will find the very thing that angers you. You may have to look a while, but you will find it.

For example, I once became irritated with Linda because I thought she was whining while explaining something to me. She seemed tearful, and I despised whiners—I who had explored the world on motorcycles, parachuted, climbed mountains, and led top-secret missions to top-secret places. But I asked myself why I had become irritable, and I began to observe myself as carefully as I could. Two months later, while explaining something to Linda, I suddenly heard myself pleading like a child!

I was exhilarated because I had discovered a part of my personality I did not know about, and I began to challenge it. I learned to identify the physical sensations I felt just before I whined, which were always painful, and I practiced remaining silent instead of whining. The more I practiced, the less I whined.

I'M SURE IT IS YOU

Think of someone you don't like. Identify exactly what you dislike, for example:

- Her stinginess

- His loud boasting

- Her lack of integrity

Note these characteristics in your journal. Be specific. Now, look within yourself to find the same characteristics.

Be patient with yourself. This may take some time.

Write what you learn about yourself in your journal.

The behavior of others is never an issue in your spiritual growth, but your emotional reaction always is. Painful emotions are signals from your soul that remind you to stop and experience what you are feeling before you choose a response.

Painful emotions
are signals
from your soul
that remind you to
STOP
and
EXPERIENCE
what you are feeling.

Your purpose on the Earth is to become a personality that creates with the intentions of your soul. As you learn how to do that, using your sense of meaning as an inner compass to distinguish between authentic and artificial needs, you move toward your potential as a flower grows toward the sun.

" You move toward your
fullest potential."

The intentions of your soul are harmony, cooperation, sharing, and reverence for Life.

PART 4

Choice and Power

17

HARMONY

After World War II, warring cultures in an eastern
part of Europe were united under a Communist dictator and lived together without conflict. Their lack of
conflict appeared as harmony, but actually deep hatreds ran
beneath the surface, unable to be expressed in a police state.
Neighbors thought hostile thoughts, cultivated old feuds, and
held cruel judgments.

The secret police, national militia, and Soviet Army com-
bined to prevent these hatreds from surfacing. Political dis-
sention was not permitted, and only speeches that supported
Communist goals were allowed. Radio, television, and the press
were united under government control in a façade of harmony.
The hostile factions temporarily disappeared into a Communist
state that was held in place by force and fear. That state disinte-
grated when the Soviet Union collapsed and the dictator died.
NATO sent missions, parliaments formed committees, and the

American congress debated as old hatreds produced atrocities that even hardened soldiers found unnerving.

The old cultures rose from the ashes of the Soviet empire with their agendas and hatreds intact. Like dogs, they rose snarling and tearing at one another, maiming and killing without mercy. Bosnians, Croatians, and Serbs resumed a history that the brief appearance of Communism had temporarily interrupted. The harmony that was imposed externally could not prevent the animosity that boiled beneath it from exploding. That harmony was not harmony, but a coexistence of collectives and individuals striving for survival in a police state.

That is much the same kind of harmony that exists in countless workplaces, schools, and families. They are façades of harmony in which necessities can be accomplished. These arrangements are for co-working, co-researching, co-producing, and co-living, but they are not harmony. Bonds between individuals are held in place by the need to complete a project. Sometimes mutual care develops, but the full expression of it is not allowed any more than the mutual contempt of hostile cultures was permitted in the Soviet Union.

In order to create harmony with another person, you must care enough about that person to hear her story, share her struggles, and be with her while the parts of her personality that are frightened come to the surface. Harmony requires that you accept another individual as a personality whose life is as complex and difficult as your own. You cannot open yourself only to the parts of a person that are loving, and expect to create harmony. You must also be willing to interact with the parts that are angry, jealous, vengeful, and violent.

It is easy to create harmony with someone who cares for you, but it is difficult when that person is angry, disdainful, or judgmental.

Harmony only with those who look, think, speak, and act like you is not true harmony, but the maintenance of a clique. Sometimes the clique is small, with only a few people to re-enforce one another's beliefs and perceptions. For example, they all ride motorcycles, have children, or are artists. They are harmonious because they limit their interactions to mutually acceptable areas of interest. Sometimes the clique is very large, such as the cliques of people who feel comfortable only with those who attend their church, synagogue, or mosque.

Harmony only
with those
who
look, think, speak, and act
like you
is a clique.

A nation can be a clique of millions of individuals who feel superior or entitled to what others do not have because of their nationality. Skin color, sex, education, and economic status are all foundations of cliques. Within the clique, harmony exists only as long as interactions remain nonthreatening.

REAL HARMONY?

Remember a time when you were in a difficult situation with another person. Did you create harmony? Ask yourself these questions:

- Did I say or do something to make that person feel better, even though it wasn't true?
- Did I do something so I could feel better?
- Was my feeling of well-being dependent on that person agreeing with me?
- Did I say what I needed to without blame and anger?

Note what you discovered about yourself and about harmony.

Your soul wants harmony with all of Life—with those you consider your friends and those you consider your enemies.

*Your soul
wants HARMONY
with those you consider
YOUR FRIENDS
and with those you consider
YOUR ENEMIES.*

It is as difficult to create harmony with friends as it is with adversaries because friends bring the frightened parts of their personalities into their interactions, just as you do. That makes it difficult to say no to a friend and to hear no from a friend. When you try to please another person, you distort your behavior in order to make that person comfortable, and you put yourself in a position that is not authentic. When your strategy works you become resentful, and when it fails you become angry.

Harmony requires integrity. You cannot control whether other people are authentic, but you can decide whether or not you will be. In other words, harmony with another is not always possible, but the in-tention to create it is. For example, when a friend asks for a favor and you do not feel comfortable saying no, you must choose between your discomfort and your integrity. If you say yes, you are not truly a friend to that person, because you do not care enough about him—or yourself—to say what is important to you. Not only do you fear losing your friendship, you fear asking yourself if it is, indeed, a friendship.

On the other hand, when you are not willing to accept an authentic answer, your relationship is also based in fear. You keep a record of how much you have done for her and how much she

"... when the record becomes unbalanced, the relationship breaks."

has done for you, and when the record becomes unbalanced, your relationship breaks.

FRIENDSHIP AND HARMONY

When you find yourself in an uncomfortable situation with a friend, ask yourself these questions to see if harmony is really what you want to create:

- "Am I doing or saying something to make my friend feel better, even though it isn't true?"

- "Am I doing or saying something so I can feel better about myself?"

- "Does my feeling of well-being depend on my friend agreeing with me?"

- "If my friend becomes angry and won't speak to me, will I still feel my in-tention is to create harmony?"

An in-tention is not an expectation. Harmony and expectations cannot coexist. An in-tention does not depend on what others do, but an expectation does. When others do as you expect, you are pleased, and when they do not, you feel disappointed, betrayed, or devalued. **Relationships are intimate arenas in which you encounter frightened parts of your personality and frightened parts of the personalities of others. Harmony is the in-tention to heal.**

How you express integrity is important. If you need to become angry in order to say no, or reject before you can be rejected, you cannot create harmony. Harmony requires the ability

"... you become like a deeply rooted tree that can stand in the strongest wind."

to say no, yes, or perhaps with the in-tention of creating a caring, constructive, and joyful relationship. Some circumstances call for a direct, or blunt, response, while in others, a more gentle communication is appropriate. When your in-tention is to create harmony, you become like a deeply rooted tree that can stand in the strongest wind. You do not hold expectations, but rather do what you do because you have chosen that course for yourself.

Harmony requires courage. For example, if you care for another, you will not allow him to speak to you disrespectfully, even though looking the other way or making excuses for him may appear to be the easier route. Speaking from your heart, without judgment and without expectation, is not always easy. At other times, the in-tention to create harmony without speaking is appropriate. At all times, courage and integrity are required.

Several years before we met, Linda was in a relationship with a man named Tom. They saw each other as often as possible for two years. He was an artist and had traveled the world. He was English and she loved his accent. She was fascinated and in love.

Everything changed dramatically when an acquaintance, whom she met at the same time she met Tom, came to visit. She had not seen the woman for two years, and the acquaintance did not know of Linda's relationship with Tom. Before Linda could tell her, the acquaintance began to share news of her life and mutual friends. In passing, she mentioned that Tom had recently ended an engagement to another woman. Linda was too shocked to speak. She had never felt pain of such intensity, especially in her solar plexus and chest areas. If she had not known its cause, she might have thought she was dying. She did not tell the acquaintance about Tom or the shame she was feeling, and the acquaintance left unaware of the relationship.

After what seemed like a lifetime of pain, Linda began to notice how fragile she felt, as if she might shatter. Yet at the same time she felt a soft, glowing warmth in her chest. Then she began to see her experience with Tom as a gift! She felt her pain of betrayal fully, and she remembered other times and other people with whom she was the betrayer. She wondered if there might have been more such instances in other lifetimes. The betrayed and the betrayer changed roles and changed back again. She had played both. A process completed itself within her.

The experience of healing was enormous, but when, a day later, she heard Tom's car in her driveway, she wondered how she could see him. She still felt very fragile, but the thought occurred to her that the Universe would not ask more than she could do. She set the in-tention to create harmony and continue her healing, and she went to meet Tom.

As she saw him, she realized that she loved him, but in a very different way. She told him quietly that she knew he had been engaged while she thought they were in a monogamous rela-tionship. She told him she loved him and that she was grateful for the gift she received from her experience. She also told him that integrity was important to her, and that she could not relate with him as before because she could not trust him.

As she spoke, she felt liberated. The words *the truth shall set you free* seemed to run through her, thrilling her. None of her old habits were left, and she did not need to pretend to understand Tom's behavior. There were no hurt feelings to nurse for years. There was no one to blame.

She knew that Tom would not understand everything she was saying, and she did not need him to. She was at peace with Tom, and she still is. She learned to create harmony.

Creating harmony does not require you to become a door-mat for others. In fact, it demands that you do not, because when you make yourself a doormat, people will clean their shoes on you. Creating harmony requires the courage to fail the expectations of others, to object when you feel an objection is appropriate, and to say no, yes, and maybe, without expectation.

The creation of harmony is spiritual activism. You devote your energy to what you believe, but you do not make others wrong, tolerate violence, or contribute to it, nor do you confuse kindness with weakness, or need with love.

SPIRITUAL ACTIVISM

When you interact with those who disagree, especially those with whom you very much disagree, ask yourself . . .

- "Are my in-tentions to manipulate or to create harmony?"
- "Do I revere my adversary as much as my ally?"
- "Am I making anyone a villain?"
- "Am I opposing people instead of behaviors or policies?"

If any of your answers is yes, look again at your words and actions, and start again.

The parts of your personality that object to harmony object also to your spiritual growth. They judge, condemn, and refuse to forgive. They forget that others exist.

Harmony is the conscious creation of a loving world. The in-tention to create harmony is medicine for deep pain. It opens you, illuminates your dark places, brings peace to them, and allows you to develop your greatest gift—an open heart.

*"your greatest gift—
an open heart"*

18

COOPERATION

M Y FIRST JOB IN the U.S. Army was a rifleman, the lowest ranking soldier in the infantry. The mission of the infantry is to close with and kill or capture the enemy. That was my mission, and I trained for it. I went to basic infantry training, advanced infantry training, Infantry Officer Candidate School, and then into one specialized training program after the other. I never stopped training, except when I was using my training. That happened in Vietnam.

I learned how to cooperate with my squad members. We each had our own training and jobs to do. Individually, we could not accomplish much in the way of closing with and killing or capturing an enemy, but together we were more effective. We cooperated with one another and with the other squads in our platoon. Our platoon was part of a company, which was part of a battalion, which was part of yet larger units. The larger the unit, the more individuals were involved, the greater was the need for cooperation, and the more effective it became in accomplishing the mission of the infantry.

Cooperation meant learning how to communicate and carry out orders. We were not responsible for thinking about our orders, evaluating them, or improving them. We were responsible only for following them. As each of us followed our orders, we became a unit working smoothly, usually, toward a common goal. I liked my training, mission, and the camaraderie of the army. I liked cooperating—doing my part to accomplish an objective that fit into a larger picture. I did not create the larger picture. Other people did that. It was my responsibility to follow my orders—to cooperate with them.

My last job in the U.S. Army was Executive Officer of a Special Forces (Green Beret) "A" Detachment with twelve men. My mission was to gather intelligence on North Vietnamese and Viet Cong activities in the countries neighboring Vietnam, and to execute operations against them. Both jobs appealed to me because they made me feel important and admirable. They required training and cross-training. My team trained local natives and we took them on operations with us. We needed to cooperate with each other and with them. Our training became more precise, our missions more dangerous, and our need for cooperation more important.

Each of us depended upon the others for our lives. This was the case in the infantry, too, but with only eleven men to rely upon, cooperation became the ground on which we all stood or fell. We did not necessarily like one another. We had different goals in life and different ways of attaining them. All of us had volunteered to be where we were, but none of us had known

*"...your common goals bring you
together and keep you together."*

one another when we volunteered. I volunteered for the Special
Forces, not for duty with particular individuals.

Individuals in the army are replaceable. My A Team required
different positions, such as Light Weapons Noncommissioned
Officer, Communications Noncommissioned Officer, Medic, and
Executive Officer. These positions were filled by individuals, but
the individuals were not as important to the army as their functions. Their functions were very important. We worked together
closely because our mission and our lives depended upon our
cooperation, but our common bonds were our mission and survival. They were the reasons we cooperated.

The workplace is like that, also. Your immediate survival does
not depend upon cooperating with team members, but your
common goals bring you together and keep you together. You
need to pay your rent or mortgage, buy food, and support your
family. Your company needs to sell its products or services,
and you are trained to do one of its jobs. That training requires
you to cooperate with other employees. Even if you work

mostly alone, you need to communicate and coordinate your activities.

You did not know your fellow employees, or most of them anyway, before you began work, and you probably did not know your employer. Whether or not you actually like all of your colleagues is irrelevant to your need to cooperate, because your common needs and objectives are the glue that keeps you together. Without that, you may or may not choose to continue the associations that your work requires.

Schools are also like that. You did not know most, or any, of your classmates when you enrolled. You have your objectives and they have theirs. The school has its objective, also, and the jobs of teachers, administrators, and maintenance people depend upon accomplishing it. You are all in the same building or on the same campus and cooperating enough to accomplish your separate goals. The people you meet share your goals. They want an education, or they want to provide one. That is the tie that binds you to each other. When you graduate, you may keep in touch with some of them, or you may not.

Every collective endeavor is like this. Individuals assemble in the service of a common goal and cooperate to accomplish it. They come together to elect a representative, senator, or president. They combine their creativity to protect forests or profit from them. They form neighborhood groups and professional associations. When their common goal has been gained or lost, they separate. The campaign team disbands after the election, or the professional person changes careers and joins another association, or children graduate and their parents no longer volunteer for school committees.

This is the five-sensory understanding of cooperation: the coordination of efforts to accomplish a common goal. Americans think of barn-raisings as a symbol of cooperation. They like the image of pioneer farmers helping a neighbor accomplish a goal he cannot accomplish alone. They value neighbors helping neighbors, thereby enhancing the probability of survival for all. No one in the eighteenth century could build a barn alone, yet every farm needed a barn. Helping others helps oneself. That is the picture. It is a picture of five-sensory humanity in pursuit of its fundamental goal—survival.

Some cultures think of centuries-long cathedral or mosque construction as symbols of cooperation, while others use military images. Whether coordinating the construction of cathedrals or the deployment of troops, cooperation is the same for every five-sensory collective—the voluntary combination of individual efforts in the service of a common goal. The common goal is the center of the circle, the magnet that attracts the iron filings, and the sun around which the planets revolve. Without the common goal, the sun ceases to shine, the magnet no longer attracts, and the circle falls apart.

Multisensory humans strive to create authentic power—to align their personalities with their souls. They do not need the cooperation of others to accomplish that, and others do not need their cooperation to create authentic power. **The pursuit of authentic power is not a collective endeavor.** For example, you cannot call upon a neighbor to ease the pain of your jealousy. A friend can divert your attention, but the pain of your jealousy will return again and again until you find it and pull it out by the roots. You can find new companions who do not trig-

"Your spiritual path is for you alone to walk."

ger your jealousy, but eventually your jealousy will return and you will have to find new friends again. No committee or association can ease the torment of your depression or the agony of your violent fantasies. **Your spiritual path is for you alone to walk,** and the spiritual paths of others are for them to walk because each has his work to do, and only you can do yours.

Cooperation is a tool for multisensory humans, too, but their goal is different than it is for five-sensory humans. The goal of five-sensory humans is survival, while the **goal of multisensory humans is spiritual growth.** Multisensory humans use interactions with others to help them learn about their own personalities, see their experiences as opportunities to create authentic power, explore their emotions, and observe their reactions—both when they are under stress and when they are not. In other

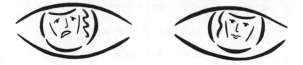

"They observe their reactions when they are under stress and when they are not."

words, they look for ways to change the parts of their personalities that create painful emotions, and ways to cultivate the parts that are wholesome and balanced.

That is cocreation. Five-sensory humans bring their education, training, and abilities to a common endeavor, but their perception is limited to what the five senses can detect, and so are their goals. **Multisensory humans bring emotional awareness, responsible choice, intuition, trust in the Universe, and their in-tention to create authentic power to their common endeavors.** Their goal is more than the five senses can detect. For example, when five-sensory humans cooperate to bring food to the hungry, they feel successful when the food has been distributed.

Multisensory humans require more, because they know their goal is not as important as how they accomplish it. For example, if they argue among themselves, judge one another, and struggle for control, they increase rather than reduce the causes of hunger. They know that hunger results not merely from a shortage of food, because humankind can grow enough food to feed itself and distribute it globally. The consciousness of hoarding, competition, discord, and exploitation creates hunger, and so the challenge is to cooperate, share, create harmony, and revere Life.

Multisensory humans
know their goal
is not
as important as
HOW
they accomplish it.

I enjoyed my self-image while I was in the army because I saw myself as courageous and admirable. People who opposed the war in Vietnam liked their self-images, too, because they also saw themselves as courageous and admirable. As individuals, we were at war for the same reasons—to feel valuable, worthy, and lovable—even though we appeared to be very different. I fought an enemy and they fought an enemy. I in-tended to win my war against a government, and they in-tended to win their war against a government.

We were brothers and sisters, but we did not know it. People at war have no compassion for their adversaries and they do not cooperate with their adversaries. They condemn them, are righteously violent, and have only tactics, strategies, defeats, and victories. The anti-war movement was a war, just like mine, and as such, it did not reduce conflict in the world. For most, it in-creased it.

Only in-tention can create a war and only in-tention can end one. Those who opposed the war in Vietnam without blame, without judgment, and with care for all involved did not con-tribute to war. Those who became angry, righteous, intolerant, and violent became what they opposed. They in-tended war, they created war, and their cooperation fed the flames of war. They distinguished between their war and the war in Vietnam, but they could not distinguish between war and peace—between the pursuit of external power and the pursuit of authentic power.

Multisensory humans in-tend to create authentic power. I cooperated with my colleagues to win my war, but I did not in-tend to create authentic power. I had another agenda—to prove myself valuable. The anti-war activists who were righteous, intolerant, and judgmental, like I was, cooperated to win their war, too, but they did not in-tend to create authentic power, either. They had their agenda. We both pursued external power—the ability to manipulate and control.

The cooperation your soul seeks has a different goal.

19

COCREATION

MULTISENSORY HUMANS COOPERATE to contribute to Life, and to create experiences that are worthy of their time on the Earth. This type of cooperation is a cocreation—it inspires all, harms none, is deeply satisfying, and requires from each the in-tention to create authentic power. Five-sensory cooperation requires only your skills.

Multisensory
COOPERATION
requires the
IN-TENTION
to create
AUTHENTIC POWER.

COOPERATING

This is an experiment to do with someone who is important to you. Let the other person know that you are experimenting with how to cooperate and would like to invite him or her to be your special friend to experiment with.

Make an appointment to do something together that is meaningful to both of you. For example:

- Cleaning out areas of unconsciousness in each other's homes together.

- Volunteering for meaningful work in your community.

- Enjoying nature.

- Going somewhere neither of you have been before.

- Helping a friend or elderly person with something he or she needs.

Allow sufficient uninterrupted time together. Set your in-tention to cocreate this activity with your friend. Your goal is not simply to complete the task, but to use your time together consciously to grow spiritually.

Notice what choices you make and the in-tentions behind your choices.

Write your discoveries about cooperation and spiritual growth in your journal. Did you forget now and then that you were experimenting? What did you learn about yourself?

You can resent, judge, and envy colleagues while cooperating with them, but you cannot cocreate with them until you appreciate them as fellow souls. In other words, you cannot cocreate while you are seeking advantage, or are angry, envious, resentful, or vengeful.

Cocreation requires the courage to examine and change yourself. In the process, you become more vulnerable, accepting, and forgiving, and people become more important to you than your goals. You support each other because you want to, not because your goal requires it.

When you cooperate to achieve a goal, the goal determines your colleagues, as it does in business, government, the military, education, etc. Multisensory humans choose their goals, but they also choose their colleagues. The Seat of the Soul Foundation, a nonprofit corporation that Linda and I cofounded, is an example. Its mission is to help individuals create authentic power. All the senior employees relocated from different parts of the country to work with this foundation because creating authentic power is their most important goal, and they want to work with colleagues who are committed to creating authentic power. Promotions, stock options, and relationships that do not nourish are not enough for them. They use their circumstances to grow spiritually, or they create new circumstances.

Cooperation to achieve only goals creates competition. For example, election campaigns generate opposing campaigns, organizations that support public schools generate organizations that support private schools, etc. All in-tend to succeed. These goals may seem valid, but if you need to win to feel better than others, you inhabit a world of winners and losers, and your self-worth depends upon being the winner. It is painful not to win, and to ease the pain, you try again. That is competition.

When you run your race, write your book, or anything else to do your best, your joy comes from engaging Life fully, without reservation or distraction. You forget your fears and your life is joyful. You appreciate the other team or the other author, and you cheer them to their best. Can you imagine such a life?

Competition and war grow from the same seed—the intention to create external power. The only difference between competition and war is the amount of violence allowed. In war, there is no limit. When family members, corporations, and nations compete, they engage each other as enemies, whether or not they think of themselves in that way. The in-tention of an individual to impose values and beliefs on another individual is identical in nature to the in-tention of a nation to impose its economics and ideology on another nation. When you compete, you plant the seed of war. When you cocreate, you plant the seed of peace.

When you
COMPETE
you plant the seed of
WAR.
When you
COCREATE
you plant the seed of
PEACE.

Cocreators know their creative power, in-tend to use it wisely, and take responsibility for their creations.

COOPERATE FOR A DAY

Think about how you can cooperate with others today. For example:

- Use what you are doing with others as an opportunity to learn about yourself.

- Notice your reactions, such as anger, resentment, jealousy, and judgment.

- As you interact, ask yourself:

  o "What is my in-tention?"

  o "Am I creating cooperation or am I competing?"

  o "Am I cooperating to feel better about myself or to please someone else?"

  o "Is my desire to cocreate?"

  o "Am I interested in the people I am with as much as in what I am doing?"

Write what you discover about yourself in your journal.

Competition focuses outward on what can be accomplished in the domain of the five senses. **Cocreation requires an inward focus on parts of the personality that need to be healed.**

External power can be won, lost, stolen, or inherited. For example, the winner of one election may not win the next; the strongest man today will not be the strongest in twenty years, and the wealthiest woman may be poor tomorrow. Authentic power cannot be lost or stolen, and no one can take it from you. Until you create authentic power, winning will be important to you—whether a gold medal, an argument, or a market share—because your self-worth is at stake.

COOPERATION VS. COCREATION

Five-sensory Cooperation	_Multisensory Cooperation_
Pursue external power	_Create authentic power_
Goal most important	_People most important_
See colleagues as coworkers	_See colleagues as souls_
Work to achieve goal	_Learn about self_

When you do not value yourself, you need others to value you and you place your worth in their hands. In other words, the less an individual values himself, the more he needs to win, or at least compete, but the real need is to be accepted, to be loved, and to contribute. Competition cannot fill these needs. Even if you win every gold medal the world has produced, you will fear losing the next.

AM I COMPETING?

Ask yourself:

- "Do I get jealous when others are invited to a party and I am not?"

- "Do I feel superior to people who don't have as much as I do?"

- "Do I get pouty when others get more attention?"

- "Do I always have to win (or won't play unless I can)?"

- "Do I feel I am more valuable or less valuable than others?"

- "Do I have to have the last word?"

- "Do I argue frequently?"

If you answered yes to any of the above, parts of your personality are competing.

Think of similar questions to ask yourself, and write your responses in your journal.

Cocreation is the conscious contribution of creativity and effort toward a common goal with the in-tention to grow spiritually in the process.

The life of Mahatma Gandhi is an example of cocreation because Gandhi included *everyone* in his cocreation. His goal was to remove the British from India. The British government ridiculed him, attacked him, and then imprisoned him, yet Gandhi continued to consider the British friends. For example, he stopped a strike to prevent a British business from bankruptcy, and he asked the British governor not to allow his political activities to "stand between us as men." In London, Gandhi stayed with textile workers who were unemployed because Indians were boycotting English cloth—and the workers cheered him! In the end, cheering British soldiers left India with Indians cheering at the dock—a shared camaraderie. Gandhi saw everyone as a fellow soul and, eventually, millions of people saw him that way, too.

Do you have the courage to cocreate?

20

SHARING

THE OLD MAN STOOD on the stage, his robes reaching almost to the floor. He looked as though he had been transported from a monastery in twelfth-century China. His head was larger than most, and his short, gray hair made his big face seem even bigger. He stood erect, yet relaxed, and I suspected that he was older than he appeared. As he spoke, a young woman translated his Mandarin words into English. I sat amazed at the depth of his thoughts and the clarity with which he spoke, even through translation. He offered insights without pomposity. He laughed often and, once, he cried. The people around me listened quietly, absorbing his ideas, or at least storing them for consideration later. As I gazed around me, I felt I could have been among a group of monks listening quietly instead of an American audience in casual clothes.

His talk flowed effortlessly, except to pause for the translator.

It seemed to me he spoke in a monotone, but my mind was alive with his ideas and my heart was full. I wondered if he shared his thoughts in this way frequently. Almost as if the man had heard my thoughts, he paused and the translator spoke into the silence:

> *Even for ten thousand ounces of gold*
> *I would not sell the way,*
> *But I will give it for free right at the crossroad*
> *If you can hear my sound.*

That talk occurred more than two decades ago, but I still remember his words. I can still see him on the stage, and I can still feel his presence. I have heard many talks before and since then. Some were by teachers, others by clergy, hundreds by television personalities, and thousands by newscasters. Through years of school and college, I listened to many speeches and lectures, some of them brilliant. Why do I remember this particular talk more clearly and more often than any other? Why do I not recall most of the thousands of other talks I have heard?

I remember that old man because he gave me a gift. He was vulnerable. I had never before seen a speaker cry during a talk. He laughed as well, and I knew that his laughter was real. After the talk, I asked the translator if the old man were reciting a poem when he spoke about ten thousand ounces of gold. "Oh, no," she told me. "He speaks without notes, and I translate what he says as he speaks." At that moment, I realized that the old man had meant what he said, and that I was at the crossroad. His words were appropriate for me. He meant them, and he shared them. He gave me a gift that he would not sell at any price.

Can you give what is precious to you? How often do you

share the best that you have? What is the best that you have? What you share is important, but why you share it is even more important.

When one of our granddaughters woke on her first Christmas morning, the family gathered around the tree to be with her. She did not realize why we were with her, or that this morning was different.

I saw her first and after we hugged, I gave her a small string of beads. She was fascinated, and her awe delighted us. She lived in the moment and it was complete for her, but we were not complete. We distracted her attention from the beads and directed it to piles of wrapped boxes at the base of the tree.

With our help, she unwrapped the first. It was a large plastic toy that moved and made noises. After that came another and then another, each with something brighter or softer or louder inside. She moved from one box to another, removing paper faster and faster until she was tearing wrapping off as quickly as she could. Her squeals got louder and longer. At first they were sounds of joy, but they soon turned into something else. She could not comprehend the magnitude of her experience. Colors, sounds, movement, and adults competed for attention. As her frustration increased, so did the volume and intensity of her squeals.

At last she became irritable and began to cry. We had taken too many pictures, called her name too many times, given her too many packages, and expressed our delight too often. It was overwhelming. Her first Christmas had become painful, and, more than that, set a precedent for future Christmas morning rituals—all having to do with unwrapping boxes one after another. The special Christmas morning had been for us. Our granddaughter had been delighted, content, and complete with the beads. The least expensive and simplest gift had been sufficient for her, but it was not sufficient for us.

We had continued past the point of her delight to satisfy ourselves, not her. In that sense, our giving to the child whom we love so dearly was not giving at all. It was taking and it left her exhausted, irritable, and confused. We needed to see her smile and laugh. We needed to shop and choose and bring home special gifts, and we needed to see our efforts rewarded with her joy. We needed this child, less than a year old, to see us as bringers of joy and happiness. She experienced us as that, but also as many conflicting things as well. She engaged the long process of finding what adults want and how to provide it for them, just as we strove to discover what our granddaughter wanted and how to provide it for her.

Sharing is a deeper dynamic. It requires knowing your intentions. We were not aware of our in-tentions. We thought we simply wanted to shower a child with love, but we also wanted to shower ourselves with love.

---

*Sharing
requires knowing your
in-tentions.*

When expectations accompany your gift, you pursue external power. Your gift is a means to an end and the end is for you, not the one who receives the gift. We wanted our granddaughter to react the way we envisioned, and for the most part, she did. Now she expects gifts at Christmas and tears paper off boxes as soon as she gets them. We did not envision that reaction, or want to create it. We wanted to express our love. We knew some of our in-tentions, but we did not know all of them.

STRINGS ATTACHED

Remember a time when you gave a gift and you were upset at the response you received. Go back to that experience in your memory. Notice what physical sensations you feel in your solar plexus, chest, and throat areas. If the sensations are not immediately apparent, keep looking for them.

Ask yourself:

- "What was my in-tention in giving this gift?"
- "Was it truly a gift?"
- "Did I have a hidden agenda?"

If you do not know all of your in-tentions before you share, you will discover them after you share, because you will become disappointed, angry, or in other ways upset if your gift is thrown away or not appreciated. Reactions such as these tell you that you had an in-tention you were unaware of or that you knew about but did not share. In other words, your internal experiences will inform you when you have a hidden agenda. Your gift might even be quite important to the person who receives it, such as money to go to college, but if you are disappointed with her reaction, you will know that recognition, appreciation, or obligation was your hidden objective. Otherwise, you would not feel disappointed, resentful, or angry when she is displeased with or discards your gift.

The pain of feeling unappreciated or unloved is not caused by a response to your gift, but by a part of your personality that does not feel lovable and wants others to make it feel lovable. It is a part that does favors, provides help, and gives gifts. It seeks love in all of these ways and becomes upset when it does not get it.

A REAL GIFT?

Before you give a gift ask yourself these questions:

- "Do I expect my gift to be appreciated?"
- "Do I expect to be recognized?"
- "Do I feel the person I give my gift to owes me?"
- "What would I feel if the person who received my gift gave it away? Threw it away? Didn't like it?"
- "What is my in-tention for giving this gift?"

Write what you discover in your journal.

When you insist that others accept an idea or a belief that is important to you, a part of your personality is frightened and wants to be accepted and loved. You may not feel frightened, but the need to have others think as you do comes from your fear, not from your interest in them. The more frightened you are, the more you need others to accept your idea or belief, and you see yourself as one who knows more. You are certain your path is the correct one, and you strive to convince others because you need them to validate your idea or belief. If they agree, you are content. If they do not, you feel the need to speak longer, discuss more, and explain better. Nothing can satisfy you except their agreement.

In this case, you do not have the ability to honor the path of another because you are frightened to look too closely at your own. You fear your inner doubts and the rejection of colleagues. You need others to validate your position because you are not sure it is entirely your own, and so you push forward, telling yourself that you—not they—are responsible for their well-being.

The more you need people to agree with you, the less open you are to what they think, feel, and believe. You cannot share with them because you are trying to change them, and they cannot share with you because you are not listening.

That is not sharing. That is the pursuit of external power.

ARE YOU REALLY SHARING?

What is so important to you that you need to share it frequently? For example:

- Your diet

- How you exercise

- The way your boss is wrong

- Your political beliefs

What are you certain you are right about, for example:

- Your political beliefs

- Your religious beliefs

- Your economic beliefs

- Your understanding of a certain subject

How do you feel if others don't accept what you say or believe?

Write what you learned about yourself and sharing in your journal.

21

THE GREATEST GIFT

THE PARTS OF YOUR PERSONALITY THAT ARE FRIGHTENED HOARD ANYTHING THEY FEEL WILL BENEFIT THEMSELVES, WHETHER IT IS KNOWLEDGE, AFFECTION, SPARE PARTS, OR FOOD. No matter how much they have, they fear not having enough—for example, enough time to complete a project so they become angry when interrupted, or enough affection so they become jealous when others receive it, etc. The scarcity they fear is not in their future, but in their present. It surrounds them, and they continually react to it.

Animals store food for winter, but they do not store more than they need. We accumulate for the future also, but when our needs appear to grow continually, what we accumulate continually appears inadequate. The solution is not to increase our accumulation, but to assess more accurately what is needed—this is difficult when you are frightened.

Businesses strive to increase a surplus called profit, which is divided among investors who continually demand more. Resources, information, and talent are hoarded to meet these demands. Trade secrets are defended, markets are cornered, and mailing lists are guarded. Nothing is given, except when it creates profit, and everything is taken because no profit is excessive. Hoarding is the end and the means when business is the pursuit of external power and very few businesses are not. Like businesses, individuals also want more, fear losing what they have, and hoard to create the ability to manipulate and control each other. In other words, hoarding is a result of pursuing external power.

When scarcity exists for you internally, external abundance will not fill it. The scarcity that creates the need to hoard is a scarcity of self-value. In other words, self-disdain, self-contempt, and self-hatred cannot be healed with money, recognition, affection, attention, or influence because no matter how much you gain, the need for more is still there, like the ever-receding horizon that you cannot reach no matter how far or fast you travel.

Scarcity of
SELF-VALUE
cannot be remedied
by
Money
Recognition
Affection
Attention
or
Influence.

"Give all that you can and accept all that you are given."

Internal abundance is realizing you are worthy of your life, recognizing the potential for spiritual growth your struggles offer you, and trusting the Universe. It is also the joy of being alive, awe of your responsibility for what you create, relaxing into the present moment, and knowing that you have nonphysical assistance when you need it.

In other words, internal abundance is self-compassion and self-appreciation. You open to the world, to your life, and to others, and you give all that you can and accept what you are given.

WHEN DO YOU HAVE ENOUGH?

In what areas of your life do you feel a scarcity? For example, do you feel a shortage of any of the following:

- Time

- Friends

- Talent

- Good looks

- Money

- Love

- Attention

Make a list of what you don't have enough of.

Circle the items on your list that you are willing to look at from a new perspective. Consider each, and as you do . . .

- Notice any thoughts you have about how you don't have enough.

- Notice any painful sensations in your body, such as tight shoulders, clenched jaw, upset stomach, or pain in your chest.

- Ask yourself, "Am I willing to open to the possibility that it is my self-value that is lacking, and not what I think is lacking?"

- If yes, set the in-tention to heal the frightened parts of your personality that feel they don't have enough, and consider the possibility that you are valuable, loved, and internally abundant.

Do you feel you are developing a new perspective? Keep a log in your journal of what changes you notice in yourself.

The sun warms all and does not require appreciation or recognition. In the same way, internal abundance radiates from you like a sun.

The consequences of creativity that benefits others and the consequences of creativity that benefits only you are different because the in-tention is different. For example, a friend once declared, "I have enough food stored to feed one hundred people for a year." Actually, she had enough food to feed herself for one hundred years. When you hoard, you are motivated by frightened parts of your personality and you intend to benefit yourself. You are running on a treadmill, so a faster pace does not bring you to the finish more quickly, or even move you in that direction.

Sometimes it is easier to remain silent than to share what is difficult to say. For example, if you think you have been wronged, it takes courage to tell the one you think has wronged you. **Sharing requires you to care about the other person.** If you do not care about that person, when you are angry at him, you will indulge your anger and have no interest in truly reaching out to him, even if you spend hours explaining why you are angry.

When you share, you are motivated by healthy parts of your personality. For example, on my first audience show with Oprah Winfrey, I met a woman whose only son had been murdered. For years this woman hated the murderer and called the district attorney and the warden every month to say, "Tell me he has been killed," or "Tell me he has AIDS." Eventually, the idea of talking to the young man occurred to her, but each time she thought about it, her hatred rose again. At last, she gathered her courage and arranged a meeting.

I was sitting with Oprah in front of the cameras next to this woman when Oprah played a video tape of a meeting between the woman and the young man who murdered her son. It was her first visit to the prison. "If you had known how much I loved him," she said to the young man sitting on the other side of a table, "I know you would not have killed him. If you knew him the way I did, if you knew what he wanted to become and what a good person he was, I know you would not have killed him." As she spoke, tears began to form in his eyes, and he looked down at the table, then at her, and then at the table again. Suddenly the woman put her head on the table, her hand extended toward the young man, and began to sob. Tentatively he reached toward her hand, and then took it. The two remained that way for several seconds, the woman sobbing and tears wetting the solemn face of her son's murderer.

The woman became a regular visitor to the young man, caring for him and counseling him. Now she visits all the Texas prisons, where she speaks with young burglars, rapists, and murderers. Before each talk, she asks herself, "What would I want a mother to say to these young men if my son were one of them?" Then she lets her heart soften and speaks.

That is sharing.

It takes courage to share painful emotions with those you feel have caused them—to face the possibility of rejection—and the in-tention to create a friendship, but if you leave the distance between you that your judgment has created, you lose power.

Sharing is different from complaining, which is an attempt to make someone else responsible for your experiences. That is what the woman did when she called the district attorney and the warden. A complaint is a demand that another person change so that you will feel more comfortable. In other words, it requires someone else to act differently so that you will not have to. Sharing is a communication with the in-tention to heal yourself, create constructively, and come closer to another individual.

Even when you are frightened of what you must do to share, you are grateful for the opportunity because sharing energizes and fulfills you. When you do not share what your soul wants to share, joy leaves you, meaning becomes a stranger, and you grow rigid and brittle.

The greatest gift you have to share is your presence. When you listen with full attention, without thinking about how you are going to reply, the dinner you are planning, or your projects, you give the gift of your presence. You are aware, you feel, and you are free to choose your in-tentions and create your experiences consciously.

The greatest
gift
you can give
is
your
presence.

The more you share, the more you have to share. Images and perceptions emerge in you, guiding you and illuminating your choices. When you share your caring, patience, and open heart, you shine like the sun.

This is how your soul wants to share.

"... you shine like the sun."

22

REVERENCE FOR LIFE

FRIEND TOLD ME about a fashionable party she attended, as the guest of a friend, at an impressive mansion with beautifully manicured lawns. Servers in formal attire offered hors d'oeuvres and drinks from silver trays, beautiful food was displayed at convenient locations, and a string quartet set a lively and sophisticated mood. All this was alien and distasteful to my friend who grew up middle class with rigid judgments about people with wealth, such as, "They are ruthless, or they would not have so much," and "They exploit or they would not be so wealthy."

When the music stopped, the hostess appeared at the top of a wide spiral staircase dressed in a soft black trailing gown. Slowly she began to descend, as though floating downward, while jewels in her necklace and rings sparkled and her rich brown hair caressed her bare shoulders and accentuated her slim white arms and gloved hands. My friend's own dress suddenly seemed ordinary to her, and she felt her face flush with shame. She wanted to hide her coarse hands, and she longed for familiar friends.

As the smiling hostess descended, she seemed amused, but not at the expense of the people there. Her impish cheeks and delicate chin reminded my friend of a childhood companion, and for a brief moment, memories of playful times, secrets shared, and young girls on young adventures replaced the mansion, the hostess, and the guests. Images of grass, a large oak tree, shade, and the Midwest flooded back to her from a distant and friendly past, and she saw her favorite place, her favorite doll, and her favorite friend.

The hostess was now in the foyer and moving forward, her gown still trailing.

"Claire?" she asked tentatively. "Claire, can that be you?"

Abruptly my friend returned to the party, the mansion, and the woman with jewels and the impish smile now standing before her.

"Jennifer!" she gasped. "Jennifer! Yes, I'm Claire!" and the two women stood facing each other, radiant with the rapidly returning recognition of a friendship that predated so many struggles, disappointments, and successes. The worlds that separated them disappeared, and two childhood friends from a common place in the shade beneath an old oak in the Midwest met once again.

My friend's opinion of wealthy people disappeared as she recognized in Jennifer the same smile, now mature, of her childhood neighbor. She no longer noticed Jennifer's necklace, rings, and gown, and the mansion receded in her awareness. They spoke at length and depth about the men they married and the children they mothered, about births and deaths and illnesses and health. They grieved and laughed and made plans to meet again. The guests at the party had become friends of her dear friend, and the mansion the home of her dear friend. As joy replaced fear, Jennifer's clothes, jewels, and home became no more to Claire than scenery on a stage.

The experience of reverence is like that. You see beyond appearances, your judgments disappear, and your heart opens. In other words, your attention goes to the essence of a person or thing, and appearances become no more than costumes.

CAN YOU SEE DIFFERENTLY?

Think of a person you know with whom you don't feel close but would like to. Why do you feel distant? Do you feel inferior or fearful, or envious of your friend, or disdainful, superior, and judgmental?

Then ask yourself:

- "Have I been looking only at my friend's Earth suit?"

- "Have I been focusing on what he does?"

- "Have I been focusing on how she dresses?"

- "Do I feel I cannot communicate because of a misunderstanding or disagreement?"

- "Am I distant because my life has taken me in a different direction?"

Take whatever time you need on this exercise:

- Close your eyes and picture your friend.

- Set your in-tention to see beyond your friend's Earth suit.

- Remind yourself that you don't know all that goes into his life . . . his challenges, fears, joys, and terror.

- Remember you are a soul and your friend is a soul, also.

Open your eyes and notice how you feel about your friend now. Do you feel compassion? If not, continue this exercise until you feel a shift from seeing your friend only as a personality to knowing he is a soul wearing an Earth suit. Allow yourself to feel the instant that your fear and judgmental reaction disappear and reverence appears.

When you see a white American businessman, or a brown Mexican mother, or a yellow Buddhist farmer, you see no more than Claire saw when she saw only Jennifer's mansion, gown, and jewelry. When Claire realized that those things were not Jennifer, they lost their importance and Jennifer became important.

The essence of who you are is your soul. As you become multisensory, you begin to see yourself and others as souls first and personalities second. **Your personality is the costume your soul is wearing.** It is male or female, young or old, large or small, rich or poor, quick-witted or slow, with black, white, yellow, red, or brown skin. Your personality changes with time, and eventually it dies. When you see only appearances, you see only a costume a soul is wearing. **Reverence is seeing the soul that is wearing the costume.** It is going beyond the shell of appearances and relating to the essence of a person or thing.

Remember that all the characteristics your five senses can detect belong to a personality because you cannot see, hear, touch, smell, or taste a soul.

DEEPER THAN APPEARANCE

For this exercise, pick a day when you will be seeing many people—maybe those you know at work, some you may have met at a party, or many who are complete strangers in a restaurant, airport, or shopping center. Your assignment is to try to see each person as a soul instead of a personality. This is an inner experience. While you are doing this experiment ask yourself:

- "How am I feeling about each person?"

- "Am I remembering that each person is wearing an Earth suit that is perfect for him?"

- "Do the people that I see differently respond to me differently?"

- "If you interact, does your conversation with them have a different quality?"

Write your experiences in your journal.

If you think business people, in general, are predatory, and then you meet a businesswoman who was a friend of your mother's in their youth, her connection with your mother becomes more important to you than your judgments of business-people, and you want to know about that connection. In the same way, if you have a preconception that someone is a cold, impersonal person who should not be teaching in elementary school, and then you discover that he loves children as much as you do, you become more interested in him than in your judgment. You want to know how he teaches troubled children, sensitive children, and slow learners, and how he explains sex, race, economic differences, and drugs. In other words, you open to him.

This is the moment when fear, judgment, and disdain disappear. It is also the experience of compassion. **Compassion brings you out of your self-created isolation and into the larger world of joy and pain that is the human experience.**

When you see only personalities, compassion is harder because you focus on differences that frighten you, and you judge what you fear—such as skin color, body shape, sex, culture, religion, hair style, and anything else that is different. You can relate to appearances like your own, but even then you judge. For example, not all white people like all white people; not all black people like all black people; not all poor people like all poor people, etc. Appearances always differ, but when you see the essence beneath appearances, your judgments disappear and you create a world in which harm is not possible because your relationships become soul-to-soul.

When you see beyond appearances, you see holiness. You see colleagues, competitors, and kind, cruel, impatient, and sensitive people as holy. You also see people you like, people you do not like, and yourself as holy. You see holiness everywhere—above, below, in front, and behind.

"Holiness above, below,
in front and behind."

HOLINESS

When you wake each morning say to yourself, "I in-tend to see Holiness in every person and everything today."

Imagine what that might mean. If you forget during the day, remind yourself and set the in-tention again.

Write your experiences in your journal.

When you become aware of yourself as a soul in the Earth school, you become aware of others as souls, also, and their personalities become interesting, just as different clothing is interesting.

MY EARTH SUIT

Draw a picture of your own Earth suit. Take your time and put in every detail you can. Don't worry if you think you can't draw. This picture is for you. If you don't want to draw a picture, find a photo of yourself. Keep your drawing or your photo safe as a reminder that your Earth suit was picked by your soul for your journey through the Earth school, and that it is perfect for you.

You see the Universal law of cause and effect and the Universal law of attraction at work as personalities create consequences and attract like energy with their choices.

These are perceptions of the soul: holiness and unending opportunities to create authentic power—and reverence for Life.

PART 5

Responsible Choice

23

THE INSIDE STORY

T HIS IS A STORY many people have heard. It has been
told in every culture, and in every age. It is the story of
an individual who committed himself to a worthy goal,
pursued the goal to his best ability, and then betrayed the goal. It
is a story of pride and ambition. It is also the story of a good
in-tention and the actions that assured its destruction. The hero
is not different from you and me, and no matter how often or
where this story repeats itself, the beginning and the end are
always the same. Only the individuals who live this story change.
Perhaps you are one of those individuals.

The circumstances of the story change each time another
individual lives it, and so the telling takes different forms. The
characters also change, and so does the scenery, the culture, and
even the language the story is told in. There are countless ver-
sions of this story, but all of them—apart from the name, the
in-tention, and the location—are the same.

For convenience, we will call the hero of this story Jonathan. The hero does not need to be a male, and his or her name could be yours as well as Jonathan. If you think this story may be your story, substitute your name and circumstances for Jonathan's now and then, and see if it fits.

Jonathan was a preacher who recognized his calling early. He loved to talk about religion, cared for people, and had ambitions. He had an openness about him that made him attractive, and people enjoyed listening to him speak. His words stirred them and reminded them to care for their brothers and sisters. He also created homeless shelters and street kitchens.

People were drawn to Jonathan's vision, encouraging words, and open, supportive ways. As Jonathan's reputation reached more people, his congregation grew until it no longer fit into the building he had rented, and they built a larger building. Soon, they outgrew that one, too. They bought an auditorium and Jonathan began to talk on the radio, and then on television. When more money arrived to support Jonathan's programs, he bought a small campus and began to teach students how to explain what Jonathan taught, and to expand the programs he created.

Jonathan could not accept some things, and prostitution was one of them. The more he thought about it, the more horrible it seemed to him. He began to give sermons against prostitution, and over the years, he found himself waging a war against it. Eventually, Jonathan's war against prostitution became his best-known cause—even more so than his homeless shelters and street kitchens. He used his radio and television shows to campaign against prostitution in the most vehement ways.

Then a shocking thing happened—so shocking that even Jonathan could not believe it. Jonathan had sex with a prostitute. He was astounded. The idea of it! The absurdity of it! The shame of it! The danger of it. He returned to his life with his secret. His revulsion at what he had done grew stronger and his speeches against prostitution became more passionate. To Jonathan's horror, the idea of visiting the prostitute haunted him. He pushed her from his mind and busied himself with studies, prayer, and service, but he could not escape the thought of sex with her. It came to him at home, then in his office, and then while he was giving a sermon!

The more he resisted the idea, the more magnetic it became, and the more he fought it, detested it, and condemned it, the more it occupied his consciousness. He spoke regularly from his pulpit and organized anti-prostitution campaigns and police actions. As the intensity of his war against prostitution increased, so did his fascination with the prostitute.

At last, taking great care to avoid recognition, he visited her again. He was simultaneously fascinated and repulsed by her. The intrigue of his visits both terrified and captivated him. He felt an electricity and trembling in his body as he began each secret rendezvous with an excitement that was absent from the rest of his life. He was torn between guilt, shame, and remorse on the one hand, and exhilaration and carnal fascination on the other.

This continued for months, with Jonathan living two lives. One was moral and exemplary. The other was thrilling, dangerous, and sexual. The illicit life quickly became more attractive, more irresistible, and more dangerous. Even so, Jonathan's visits began to seem almost routine to him. He became experienced in concealing them—he knew what had to be done, and the thrill of what lay waiting for him.

Then a second shocking thing happened. Like the first, it was so shocking that Jonathan, again, could not believe it. Jonathan was seen leaving the prostitute, recognized, and photographed! "Jonathan! Wait! What are you doing here? How can you explain this?" The voice of the photographer rang in his ears as he ran for his car and sped away—away from the nightmare behind him, away from the horrible woman, away from anyone who could know what he had done.

But he could not escape his actions so easily. Pictures of Jonathan and the prostitute appeared in the newspaper the next day, and the phone began to ring incessantly. Journalists knocked at his door and waited when no one answered. Jonathan lay in bed. None of the previous night and the morning seemed real. He wanted to return to his congregation, to the people who loved him, to the life he cherished—but all was lost. More photos appeared in the newspaper, but the worst was yet to come. He could not bring himself to listen when the prostitute was interviewed on the radio, and again, when she appeared on television. The enormity of his creation was more than he could grasp, but he would have time to grasp it.

Jonathan could not reassemble the pieces of his life. The trust and admiration of his congregation were gone, and worst of all, his ability to help them, to contribute to their lives, and to share his ideas with them were gone. Everything important to him was destroyed—his integrity, his friendships, and his ability to do what he loved.

Years passed, but that episode followed him everywhere. Wherever he went, his story followed him. Like a chain around his neck, heavy for him to carry and impossible for others to ignore, it became a part of his life. When people spoke of his goodness, they also spoke of the chain. When they thought of his noble deeds, they also thought of the chain. Jonathan thought about the chain, too. He is still thinking about it.

Jonathan's inability to tolerate prostitution was a message to him that he misunderstood. He saw prostitution as evil and, like a white knight, rode forth to battle it. He fought long and hard, but he lost his battle because he fought it on the wrong battlefield. It did not occur to Jonathan that the evil he tried to fight was located within him, and so he saw and fought it elsewhere. He refused to look inside himself, and each time his attraction arose, he pushed it away in horror. Yet each time, it returned more robust and more appealing until, at last, it became stronger than he could resist and the very thing he battled engulfed him. Jonathan became what he despised most.

That is the universal story. It is a story of refusing to look inside and instead looking outside. **What you discover when you look inside are the very things you find most repulsive in others.** When you struggle against them in others—as Jonathan did—you have no chance of healing them in yourself. The more you struggle, the stronger they become because ignoring them feeds them, and they grow. They shout louder and become bolder and more determined to express themselves. Eventually, they do.

WHAT ARE YOU TEMPTED BY?

- To keep the extra money you are given by mistake?
- To have an affair with someone who is already in a relationship?
- To eat that ice cream, cake, or bag of chips when you are on a diet?
- To smoke when you have promised yourself that you will quit?
- Fudge the truth when you can get away with it?

Look carefully at yourself and make a list of what tempts you.

What you refuse to acknowledge in yourself begins to fill your thoughts and fantasies. If you ignore it, it appears in full color on the screen of your mind. That is a temptation. **Temptation brings a negativity within you to your awareness so that you can see it clearly.** It repeatedly presents the negativity so that you cannot ignore it, because each time you try, it becomes more appealing and attractive.

Temptation is a gift from the Universe that illuminates negativity in you so that you can recognize it before you act. In other words, a temptation is a chance to choose responsibly because it allows you to see what a frightened part of your personality in-tends to do so you can decide whether or not you want to do it. **A temptation is an opportunity for you to choose differently before you create destructive and painful consequences.**

It allows you to see your inside story before it becomes your outside story.

24

TEMPTATION

JONATHAN'S TEMPTATIONS came as friends to tell him what he did not want to hear but needed very much to learn about himself. The friends said, "Look clearly at what you are in-tending. It is not others who are in-tending this. It is you. Is this what you really want? Look clearly, Jonathan, and decide," but Jonathan closed the door on them.

What friends have you been ignoring? What messages are you refusing to acknowledge? Acknowledging a temptation does not mean acting on it, but rather having the courage to face the enormity of what needs to be changed in you. **A temptation is a dress rehearsal for a negative karmic event.** It shows you exactly what you refuse to acknowledge in yourself. Until then, what you will not acknowledge holds power over you, and the more you deny it, judge it, or see it as temporary, the more power it gains over you. In other words, your obsessions, compulsions, and addictions originate in you, and nowhere else. Your temptations show you how powerful they are so that you can acknowledge, challenge, and change them.

A TEMPTATION IS A DRESS REHEARSAL

Make a list in your journal of the things that tempt you or seem almost irresistible to you, such as:

- Drinking alcohol

- Eating food

- Having sex or looking at pornography

- Gambling

- Taking drugs

- Shopping

Now identify the one area that occupies most of your thoughts, images, and fantasies.

Consider these inner experiences as a private preview of what a frightened, out-of-control part of your personality is planning. Ask yourself, "Do I want to allow this part of my personality to remain out of control?"

Write what you discovered about yourself in your journal.

A temptation brings your attention to negativity within you that would create destructive consequences if it were allowed to remain unconscious, and it gives you a chance to cleanse yourself of it before you act and create painful experiences.

Temptation
shows you
what
you are
considering
so
you can
choose responsibly.

In other words, temptation allows you to locate and heal parts of yourself within your own world of energy before your actions spill over into the worlds of others and create consequences you would not want to create. Jonathan's temptation did not ruin the life he loved. Jonathan's actions did those things. He ignored his opportunity to avoid all of that, and instead denied the parts of himself that craved sex. At last, those parts stepped into his life, fascinating him, terrifying him, and destroying all that he valued.

When you use a temptation to excuse your decisions, you disempower yourself. You blame others, evil, or the Universe, and you do everything except to look inside yourself, see how powerful the frightened parts of your personality are, and change them.

When you use a
TEMPTATION
as an
EXCUSE
to do what you already
plan to do,
you
DISEMPOWER
yourself.

Temptation is not a power over you. You have the power.
Temptation merely shows you what you are considering so that
you can choose responsibly.

THE POWER OF CHOICE

The next time you are tempted:

- Stop.

- Take note of what sensations you feel in your
  solar plexus, chest, and throat areas when you
  don't act on your temptation.

- Consider the consequences of acting on your
  temptation.

- Ask yourself if you want to create those consequences.

- Remember that the power to indulge or challenge this frightened part of your personality
  is completely in your hands.

- **Remind yourself, "This temptation is not stronger than who I want to become."**

- **Choose.**

Repeat this each time you are tempted.

In other words, temptation is a decoy that draws negativity from you, and as you respond to the decoy, you cleanse yourself of that negativity by becoming aware of it instead of having to live through the experience. The Universe introduces each individual to his or her power through temptation by showing you when and how you are losing power.

The same energy that tempted Jesus, who became the Christ, with dominion over the world, and that tempted Siddhartha, who became the Buddha, with all the pleasures of the world, tempts the wife and husband to adultery, the accountant to steal, and the student to cheat. It also tempts you. **You cannot gain strength from choices that do not stretch you.**

"*...temptation is a decoy that draws negativity from you...*"

THE GIFT OF TEMPTATION

When you are tempted, say these things to yourself:

- "This is what I have refused to acknowledge about myself in the past."

- "This part of my personality is frightened and out of control."

- "This is an opportunity for me to choose differently before I create painful consequences for myself."

- "The power to say yes or no to this temptation is fully in my hands."

Temptation is a gift that allows you to choose responsibly. Use it wisely.

25

POSSIBLE FUTURES

EVERY CHOICE YOU MAKE BRINGS A POSSIBLE FUTURE INTO YOUR REALITY. When you choose without thinking about possible futures, the futures you choose are like your past, and your experiences become familiar and predictable. For example, each time you react angrily, you choose a future with distrust, resentment, and pain in it.

"Your experiences become predictable."

Your future does not have to be painful. Even if you have reacted angrily in the past, you can respond differently the next time by not speaking in anger, even while you are enraged. Each moment offers you an opportunity to bring a different possible future into your reality. Not even your nonphysical Teachers know in advance what you will choose when you become angry, or jealous, or frightened. If you have the courage to feel your anger, jealousy, or fear without acting on it, you bring a future into your life that is very different from the future that shouting, withdrawing emotionally, or using your fists would have created.

IT'S ALWAYS MY CHOICE

What behavior or reaction do you feel powerless to change in yourself, yet would be willing to experiment with choosing differently? For example, when you feel jealous, angry, or resentful, do the following:

- Remember what consequences this behavior or reaction has created for you in the past.

- Look for physical sensations in your throat, chest, and solar plexus areas and notice what thoughts you are having.

Write these things in your journal.

Follow these steps to a new choice:

- Decide what consequences you want to create in your future.

- Determine if now is the time to change this behavior/reaction.

> • If yes, set your in-tention to make a different choice.
>
> • Make a choice that will create consequences you are willing to accept responsibility for.
>
> • If you find yourself reacting again, be gentle with yourself and start this process again.
>
> Write what you discover in your journal.

You can change the possible future you will bring into your reality in any moment. When you choose possible futures of harmony, cooperation, sharing, and reverence for Life, you create authentic power.

---

*Your experiences
are not limited
to
what
you
have created
in the past.*

When I began writing *The Dancing Wu Li Masters: An Overview of the New Physics,* I was an angry, resentful, and sexually addicted young man. I raged against the world, which I felt was unjust, especially to me. I thought only about myself, and I worried mostly about paying rent, affording food, and finding sex. Because of the Universal law of attraction, my friends were also angry and resentful, and we took what we could from a world we disdained. I saw myself as an admirable and gallant victim of an uncaring world. This life was painful, but it was all I knew.

One day I was invited to a meeting of physicists at the Lawrence Berkeley Laboratory in Berkeley, California, and I decided to go. That decision brought an unexpected possible future into my reality. The physicists there discussed questions such as, "Does consciousness create reality?" Their conversations exhilarated me, but to my surprise, I discovered later that I could not re-create them, so I eagerly began to read, trying to understand what I had heard.

I went to the next meeting, and the next, until I became a regular. Slowly I began to comprehend some of the concepts that excited me so during the first meeting—such as "complementarity" and the "uncertainty principle." As I pondered the paradoxical data that confronted the founders of quantum mechanics fifty years earlier, I was surprised to discover that the development of quantum physics was unfolding in *me* as if I were there. "If THAT is so," I would say to myself, "THIS must be so!" and then discover that one of the pioneers of quantum mechanics had thought the same. Most were even younger than I was at the time they created quantum mechanics, and I felt a kinship with them.

As I read, I realized I would not remain interested in physics indefinitely, and so I decided to write a book for those who, like me, had no knowledge of science or mathematics, but wanted to understand quantum mechanics. *The Dancing Wu Li Masters* was that book, and it was also my first gift to others because, until then, I had lived my life only for me. When I wrote, I always pictured a reader who had as much or more intelligence than I and who had a deep interest in quantum physics.

I visited the physics library at the University of California at Berkeley and the used book stores near the campus often, and each time I found books that helped me understand more, and write more. Each time I worked on the book, I forgot to worry about the rent, to be angry, or to think about sex. The manuscript grew steadily for eighteen months and the day before it was published, it received a rave review in *The New York Times*. Then it won The American Book Award for Science, was reprinted by every book club, and translated into sixteen languages.

Since that time, I have become interested in people and written four books on authentic power, including those I wrote with Linda. I no longer see myself as a victim, I have explored the power of choice, and I am still exploring it. This future was unlikely for the young, angry, sexual addict who came to a meeting of physicists out of curiosity. Its probability was almost zero. Almost, but not quite.

MY PAST IS NOT MY FUTURE
(UNLESS I CHOOSE IT)

Say these words to yourself with the energy of commitment:

- "My experiences are not limited to what I have created in the past."
- "At any moment I can choose the possible future I will bring into my reality."

Write your options in your journal. Decide how you will choose differently next time. Then imagine yourself making this healthier choice, and write what you learn.

Writing *The Dancing Wu Li Masters* did not heal my anger or my addiction, but it gave me experiences of life without them. When I was not writing my fears returned, but when I wrote they disappeared again, and I was fulfilled, creative, and joyful. If I had ignored the opportunity to meet so many fine physicists, or the discoveries I made with them, or the book I was inspired to write, I would not have brought into being the future that led to my present.

I did not come to terms with my sexual addiction for another twelve years. I continue to make the best choices I can when I am angry, and in the process, anger has become a smaller part of my experience. That is how responsible choice works—decision by decision, I brought possible futures into being, and they brought me to Linda, this book, and you.

26

THE OPTIMAL CHOICE

WHEN YOU MAKE A CHOICE you walk through a doorway and it closes behind you, while other doorways that you could have chosen disappear, and new doorways appear before you. For example, if you choose to move to a new city, the opportunity to remain where you now live disappears and so do the opportunities that would have awaited you there, but in their place appear new opportunities that did not previously exist.

This is how you create the experiences of your life. Each choice offers you different opportunities, you choose one, the opportunities you did not choose disappear, and more opportunities present themselves.

You bring a future into your reality each time you make a choice, and as that future becomes your present, you must choose again. This process will not end while you are in the

" When you walk through a doorway –
make a choice – more doorways appear. "

Earth school. Each choice brings into your reality an appropriate future. For example, reacting angrily creates the consequences of anger, and responding with love creates the consequences of love, etc.

CHOOSE AGAIN

Pick an example of something you do repeatedly in your life that has painful results and that you would like to change.

Every morning, say to yourself, "Each time I react in (anger, jealousy, etc.), I create a future that is different from the one I create if I respond with (patience, kindness, etc.). What do I want to choose?"

Write in your journal what you discover about yourself.

One choice among the many that present themselves to you is the optimal choice. Whatever you choose, more choices will appear, and one of them will then be optimal. In other words, you always have the opportunity to make the optimal choice. **The optimal choice is the choice your soul wants— to create harmony, cooperation, sharing, or reverence for Life.**

When you make those choices, you come alive, your creativity flows, all that you do has meaning, all that you say is appropriate, and all that you experience is a gift. You see the perfection of your life and the lives of others, you know your life has a purpose, and you live it.

"...your creativity flows..."

CHOICE MAPS

Can you remember a choice you made that brought you to your present situation? It might have been a choice to move to a new city, get married, change jobs, go to school, etc.

Now go back one layer and try to remember the choice that allowed you to make the prior choice. For example, the choice to move to a new city might have allowed you to meet the partner you chose to marry, or the choice to change jobs might have allowed you to accept an offer to move to another city.

Go back a few more layers, and try to remember the choices you made that lay beneath the choices you have already identified.

Then construct a diagram or "Choice Map" in your journal. Start with a present circumstance, such as your location, job, or partner, and identify the choices that brought you to where you are now.

The optimal choice is the choice to create authentic power. This choice continually presents itself, and eventually you will make it. Then you will become a scientist of the soul, gain the freedom to experiment with your life, and see what works for you and what does not. That is when you begin to become aware of what you are feeling, use meaning as your guide, and recognize yourself as the creator of your experiences.

AWARENESS DAY

For the next twenty-four hours try to remain aware of your choices, moment by moment.

Ask yourself these questions each time you make a choice:

- "Am I willing to assume responsibility for the consequences this choice will create?"
- "Will this choice create harmony, cooperation, sharing, and reverence for Life?"
- "Is this the optimal choice I can make?"

Practice this as often as necessary until your awareness day becomes a life of awareness.

The creation of authentic power is a process, not an event. When you create authentic power you use your life as it was meant to be used, and that is the optimal choice, whenever and however frequently you make it. You learn about yourself, not others, change yourself, not others, and give the gifts your soul wants to give. The optimal choice is your potential calling to you, and the opportunity to make it appears continually.

The optimal choice creates constructive and empowering consequences, but every consequence you create provides you an opportunity to grow spiritually—to learn about the frightened parts of your personality and heal them—and requires you to make more choices. Sooner or later you will choose to change yourself instead of blaming others, open your heart, experience your pain, and heal it.

Sooner or later you will begin to align your personality with your soul, but only you can decide when.

INVITATION TO
THE SEAT OF THE SOUL FOUNDATION

If you are interested in learning more about authentic power, please contact The Seat of the Soul Foundation, a 501(c)3 non-profit foundation cofounded by Gary Zukav and Linda Francis. There you can:

- Subscribe to the Foundation magazine, *Soul Source*.
- Enroll in Foundation events and apply for our three year Creating Authentic Power Education.
- Take authentic power courses online.
- Join an online community of spiritual partners.
- Join a Soul Circle.
- And more.

www.seatofthesoul.org
1-888-440-7685
1-541-482-8999 (Outside USA)
welcome@seatofthesoul.org

You can also visit www.zukav.com and read the Soul Subject, Soul Question, and Soul Guest articles each month.

With love,
Gary and Linda

INDEX

ABOUT THE AUTHORS

Gary Zukav is the author of *The Dancing Wu Li Masters: An Overview of the New Physics*, winner of The American Book Award for Science; *The Seat of the Soul*, the celebrated #1 bestseller in *The New York Times, USA Today, Los Angeles Times, Publishers Weekly*, and others; and the *New York Times* bestseller *Soul Stories*. His books have sold millions of copies and are published in 24 languages. He is a graduate of Harvard and a former U.S. Army Special Forces (Green Beret) officer with Vietnam service.

Linda Francis cocreated, with Gary Zukav, the *New York Times* bestseller *The Heart of the Soul: Emotional Awareness*, and is the cofounder, with Gary Zukav, of The Seat of the Soul Foundation, a nonprofit organization dedicated to assisting individuals in the creation of authentic power—the alignment of the personality with the soul. She has been in the healing profession for three decades, first as a nurse and then as a chiropractor, and currently is cocreating curricula and co-leading events for The Seat of the Soul Foundation with Gary. They live in Oregon.